Non-Lea
Footbau
Supporters'
Guide
& Yearbook
2018

EDITOR
John Robinson

Twenty-sixth Edition

For details of our range of 2,200 books and over 300 DVDs, visit our web site or contact us using the information shown below.

British Library Cataloguing in Publication Data
A catalogue record for this book is available from the British Library

ISBN: 978-1-86223-357-7

Manufactured in the UK by T.J. International of Padstow.

FOREWORD

Our thanks go to the numerous club officials who have aided us in the compilation of information contained in this guide as well as John Mills (for photographs of the AFC Fylde and FC United of Manchester grounds), Michael Robinson (page layouts), Bob Budd (cover artwork) and Tony Brown (Cup Statistics – www.soccerdata.com). We would also like to thank Wrexham FC and Blyth Spartans FC for providing cover photographs.

Any readers who have up-to-date ground photographs which they would like us to consider for use in a future edition of this guide are requested to contact us at our address which is shown on the facing page.

The fixtures listed later in this book were released just a short time before we went to print and, as such, some of the dates shown may be subject to change. We therefore suggest that readers treat these fixtures as a rough guide and check dates carefully before attending matches.

We would like to wish our readers a safe and happy spectating season.

John Robinson
EDITOR

CONTENTS

THE VANARAMA
NATIONAL LEAGUE

Address   4th Floor, 20 Waterloo Street,
Birmingham   B2 5TB

Phone (0121) 643-3143

Web site   www.footballconference.co.uk

Clubs for the 2017/2018 Season

AFC FYLDE

Photo courtesy of John Mills @ Altius Photography

Founded: 1988
Former Names: Formed by the amalgamation of Wesham FC and Kirkham Town FC in 1988
Nickname: 'The Coasters'
Ground: Mill Farm, Coronation Way, Wesham, Preston   PR4 3JZ
Record Attendance: 3,858 (26th December 2016)

Colours: White shirts and shorts
Telephone Nº: (01772) 682593
Fax Number: (01772) 685893
Ground Capacity: 6,000
Seating Capacity: 2,000
Pitch Size: 110 × 72 yards
Web Site: www.afcfylde.co.uk
E-mail: info@afcfylde.co.uk

GENERAL INFORMATION

Car Parking: At the ground
Coach Parking: At the ground
Nearest Railway Station: Kirkham & Wesham (1 mile)
Club Shop: 6 Station Road, Kirkham   PR4 2AS
Opening Times: Monday to Saturday 10.00am to 5.00pm. Tuesday Matchdays 10.00am to 10.00pm and Saturday Matchdays 9.00am to 6.00pm
Telephone Nº: (01772) 682593 (Phone orders accepted)

GROUND INFORMATION

Away Supporters' Entrances & Sections:
No usual segregation

ADMISSION INFO (2017/2018 PRICES)

Adult Standing: £13.00
Adult Seating: £16.00
Concessionary Standing: £9.00
Concessionary Seating: £9.00
Student Standing: £5.00
Student Seating: £5.00
Under-16s Standing: £5.00 (Free of charge for members)
Under-16s Seating: £8.00 (Free of charge for members)
Programme Price: £2.00

DISABLED INFORMATION

Wheelchairs: Accommodated
Helpers: Admitted
Prices: Normal prices apply for the disabled. Helpers pay concessionary prices
Disabled Toilets: Available
Contact: (01772) 682593   (Bookings are not necessary)

Travelling Supporters' Information:
Routes: The Mill Farm Sports Village is situated by the side of the A585, just to the north of Wesham and less than a mile to the south of Junction 3 of the M55.

ALDERSHOT TOWN FC

Founded: 2013 (as a new company)
Former Names: Aldershot Town FC
Nickname: 'Shots'
Ground: Ebb Stadium, High Street, Aldershot, GU11 1TW
Record Attendance: 7,500 (18th November 2000)
Pitch Size: 117 × 76 yards

Colours: Red shirts with Blue shorts
Telephone Nº: (01252) 320211
Fax Number: (01252) 339389
Club Secretary: (01252) 320211– Bob Green
Ground Capacity: 6,500
Seating Capacity: 2,042
Web site: www.theshots.co.uk
E-mail: admin@theshots.co.uk

GENERAL INFORMATION

Supporters Club: c/o Club
Telephone Nº: (01252) 320211
Car Parking: Parsons Barracks Car Park is adjacent
Coach Parking: Contact the club for information
Nearest Railway Station: Aldershot (5 mins. walk)
Nearest Bus Station: Aldershot (5 minutes walk)
Club Shop: At the ground
Opening Times: Saturday matchdays 10.00am to 2.45pm and 9.30am to 7.30pm on Tuesday matchdays.
Telephone Nº: (01252) 320211

GROUND INFORMATION

Away Supporters' Entrances & Sections:
Accommodation in the East Bank Terrace, Bill Warren section (South Stand) – Redan Hill Turnstiles Nº 11 and 12.

ADMISSION INFO (2017/2018 PRICES)

Adult Standing: £17.00 **Adult Seating**: £19.00
Ages 11 to 16 Standing: £5.00
Ages 11 to 16 Seating: £7.00
Note: Under-11s are admitted free with paying adults – a maximum of 2 children per adult.
Concessionary Standing: £13.00
Concessionary Seating: £15.00
Note: Military personnel are charged Concessionary prices
Programme Price: £3.00

DISABLED INFORMATION

Wheelchairs: Accommodated in both the North Stand and the away section
Helpers: Admitted
Prices: £13.00 for the disabled, free of charge for helpers
Disabled Toilets: Available
Contact: (01252) 320211 (Bookings are required)

Travelling Supporters' Information:
Routes: From the M3: Exit at Junction 4 and follow signs for Aldershot (A331). Leave the A331 at the A323 exit (Ash Road) and continue along into the High Street. The ground is just past the Railway Bridge on the right; From the A31: Continue along the A31 to the junction with the A331, then as above; From the A325 (Farnborough Road): Follow signs to the A323 then turn left into Wellington Avenue. The ground is just off the 2nd roundabout on the left – the floodlights are clearly visible.

BARROW FC

Founded: 1901
Former Names: None
Nickname: 'Bluebirds'
Ground: Furness Building Society Stadium, Barrow-in-Furness, Cumbria   LA14 5UW
Record Attendance: 16,874 (1954)
Pitch Size: 110 × 75 yards

Colours: White shirts with Blue shorts
Telephone Nº: (01229) 666061
Ground Capacity: 5,045
Seating Capacity: 928
Web site: www.barrowafc.com
E-mail: office@barrowafc.com

GENERAL INFORMATION

Car Parking: Street Parking, Popular Side Car Park and Soccer Bar Car Park
Coach Parking: Adjacent to the ground
Nearest Railway Station: Barrow Central (½ mile)
Nearest Bus Station: ½ mile
Club Shop: At the ground
Opening Times: Monday to Wednesday plus Friday 9.00am to 3.00pm. Thursday 9.00am to 12.00pm and Saturday Matchdays 12.00pm to 5.00pm
Telephone Nº: (01229) 666061

GROUND INFORMATION

Away Supporters' Entrances & Sections:
West Terrace (not covered)

ADMISSION INFO (2017/2018 PRICES)

Adult Standing: £15.00
Adult Seating: £18.00
Concessionary Standing: £12.00
Concessionary Seating: £14.00
Ages 12 to 17 Standing: £5.00
Ages 12 to 17 Seating: £10.00
Under-12s Standing: £5.00
Under-12s Seating: £8.00
Note: Under-12s are admitted free with a paying adult

DISABLED INFORMATION

Wheelchairs: 6 spaces available in the Disabled Area
Helpers: Admitted
Prices: Normal prices apply
Disabled Toilets: Available
Contact: (01229) 666061   (Bookings are not necessary)

Travelling Supporters' Information:
Routes: Exit the M6 at Junction 36 and take the A590 through Ulverston. Using the bypass, follow signs for Barrow. After approximately 5 miles, turn left into Wilkie Road and the ground is on the right.

BOREHAM WOOD FC

Founded: 1948
Former Names: Boreham Rovers FC and Royal Retournez FC
Nickname: 'The Wood'
Ground: Meadow Park, Broughinge Road, Borehamwood, Hertfordshire   WD6 5AL
Record Attendance: 4,030 (2002)
Pitch Size: 112 × 72 yards

Colours: White shirts with Black shorts
Telephone Nº: (0208) 953-5097
Fax Number: (0208) 207-7982
Ground Capacity: 3,960
Seating Capacity: 1,401
Web site: www.borehamwoodfootballclub.co.uk

GENERAL INFORMATION
Car Parking: At the ground or in Brook Road car park
Coach Parking: At the ground
Nearest Railway Station: Elstree & Borehamwood (1 mile)
Nearest Bus Station: Barnet
Club Shop: At the ground
Opening Times: 9.00am to 10.00pm Monday to Thursday; 9.00am to 6.00pm at weekends
Telephone Nº: (0208) 953-5097

GROUND INFORMATION
Away Supporters' Entrances & Sections:
No usual segregation

ADMISSION INFO (2017/2018 PRICES)
Adult Standing: £18.00
Adult Seating: £18.00
Under-16s Standing/Seating: £8.50
Under-12s Standing/Seating: £4.00
Senior Citizen Standing/Seating: £13.00

DISABLED INFORMATION
Wheelchairs: Accommodated
Helpers: Admitted
Prices: Normal prices are charged for the disabled. Helpers are admitted free of charge.
Disabled Toilets: Available
Contact: (0208) 953-5097   (Bookings are not necessary)

Travelling Supporters' Information:
Routes: Exit the M25 at Junction 23 and take the A1 South. After 2 miles, take the Borehamwood exit onto the dual carriageway and go over the flyover following signs for Borehamwood for 1 mile. Turn right at the Studio roundabout into Brook Road, then next right into Broughinge Road for the ground.

BROMLEY FC

Founded: 1892
Former Names: None
Nickname: 'Lillywhites'
Ground: The Stadium, Hayes Lane, Bromley, Kent, BR2 9EF
Record Attendance: 12,000 (24th September 1949)
Pitch Size: 112 × 72 yards

Colours: White shirts with Black shorts
Telephone Nº: (020) 8460-5291
Fax Number: (020) 8313-3992
Ground Capacity: 3,300
Seating Capacity: 1,300
Web site: www.bromleyfc.tv
E-mail: info@bromleyfc.tv

GENERAL INFORMATION

Car Parking: 300 spaces available at the ground
Coach Parking: At the ground
Nearest Railway Station: Bromley South (1 mile)
Nearest Bus Station: High Street, Bromley
Club Shop: At the ground
Opening Times: Matchdays only
Telephone Nº: (020) 8460-5291

GROUND INFORMATION

Away Supporters' Entrances & Sections:
No usual segregation

ADMISSION INFO (2017/2018 PRICES)

Adult Standing/Seating: £15.00
Concessionary Standing/Seating: £10.00
Under-16s/Student Standing/Seating: £5.00
Note: Under-16s are admitted free of charge with a paying adult for advance purchases up to 1 hour before kick-off. A special £10.00 discounted price is available for Season Ticket holders of Premiership and Football League clubs.

DISABLED INFORMATION

Wheelchairs: Accommodated
Helpers: Admitted
Prices: Please phone the club for information
Disabled Toilets: Yes
Contact: (0181) 460-5291   (Bookings are necessary)

Travelling Supporters' Information:
Routes: Exit the M25 at Junction 4 and follow the A21 for Bromley and London for approximately 4 miles before forking left onto the A232 signposted for Croydon/Sutton. At the second set of traffic lights turn right into Baston Road (B265) and follow for approximately 2 miles as it becomes Hayes Street and then Hayes Lane. The ground is on the right just after a mini-roundabout.

CHESTER FC

Founded: 1885
Former Names: Chester FC and Chester City FC
Nickname: 'Blues'
Ground: Lookers Vauxhall Stadium, Bumpers Lane, Chester CH1 4LT
Pitch Size: 116 × 75 yards
Record Attendance: 5,987 (17th April 2004)

Colours: Blue and White striped shirts, Black shorts
Ground Telephone Nº: (01244) 371376
Ticket Office: (01244) 371376
Fax Number: (01244) 390265
Ground Capacity: 5,400
Seating Capacity: 4,170
Web site: www.chesterfc.com
E-mail: info@chesterfc.com

GENERAL INFORMATION

Car Parking: Ample spaces available at the ground (£2.00)
Coach Parking: Available at the ground
Nearest Railway Station: Chester (2 miles)
Nearest Bus Station: Chester (1½ miles)
Club Shop: At the ground
Opening Times: Weekdays & matchdays 10.00am–4.00pm
Telephone Nº: (01244) 371376

GROUND INFORMATION

Away Supporters' Entrances & Sections:
South Stand for covered seating and also part of the West Stand

ADMISSION INFO (2017/2018 PRICES)

Adult Standing: £15.00   **Adult Seating**: £18.00
Senior Citizen Standing: £10.00
Senior Citizen Seating: £12.00
Under-21s Seating/Standing: £10.00
Ages 16 and 17 Seating/Standing: £5.00
Under-16s Seating/Standing: £3.00 (Under-5s free)

DISABLED INFORMATION

Wheelchairs: 32 spaces for wheelchairs (with 40 helpers) in the West Stand and East Stand
Helpers: One helper admitted per disabled person
Prices: Normal prices for the disabled. Free for helpers
Disabled Toilets: Available in West and East Stands
Contact: (01244) 371376 (Bookings are necessary)

Travelling Supporters' Information:
Routes: From the North: Take the M56, A41 or A56 into the Town Centre and then follow Queensferry (A548) signs into Sealand Road. Turn left at the traffic lights by 'Tesco' into Bumpers Lane – the ground is ½ mile at the end of the road; From the East: Take the A54 or A51 into the Town Centre (then as North); From the South: Take the A41 or A483 into Town Centre (then as North); From the West: Take the A55, A494 or A548 and follow Queensferry signs towards Birkenhead (A494) and after 1¼ miles bear left onto the A548 (then as North); From the M6/M56 (Avoiding Town Centre): Take the M56 to Junction 16 (signposted Queensferry), turn left at the roundabout onto A5117, signposted Wales. At the next roundabout turn left onto the A5480 (signposted Chester) and after approximately 3 miles take the 3rd exit from the roundabout (signposted Sealand Road Industrial Parks). Go straight across 2 sets of traffic lights into Bumpers Lane. The ground is ½ mile on the right.

DAGENHAM & REDBRIDGE FC

Founded: 1992   (**Entered League**: 2007)
Former Names: Formed by the merger of
Dagenham FC and Redbridge Forest FC
Nickname: 'The Daggers'
Ground: Chigwell Construction Stadium,
Victoria Road, Dagenham   RM10 7XL
Record Attendance: 7,200 (1967 vs Reading FC)
Pitch Size: 110 × 70 yards

Colours: Red and Blue striped shirts with Blue shorts
Telephone N°: (020) 8592-1549
Office Phone N°: (020) 8592-7194
Secretary's Phone N°: (020) 8592-1549
Fax Number: (020) 8593-7227
Ground Capacity: 6,078 **Seating Capacity**: 2,233
Web site: www.daggers.co.uk
E-mail: info@daggers.co.uk

GENERAL INFORMATION

Car Parking: Street parking only
Coach Parking: Street parking only
Nearest Railway Station: Dagenham East (5 mins. walk)
Nearest Bus Station: Romford
Club Shop: At the ground
Opening Times: Monday & Tuesday 12.00pm – 4.00pm;
Thursday 12.00pm – 8.00pm; Friday 12.00pm – 6.00pm;
Saturday matchdays 1.00pm – 3.00pm.
Closed on Wednesdays, Sundays and non-match Saturdays
Telephone N°: (020) 8592-7194

GROUND INFORMATION

Away Supporters' Entrances & Sections:
Pondfield Road entrances for Pondfield Road End

ADMISSION INFO (2017/2018 PRICES)

Adult Standing: £18.00
Adult Seating: £15.00 – £21.00
Concessionary Standing: £13.00
Concessionary Seating: £10.00 – £15.00
Under-16s Standing: £10.00 (Under-10s free of charge)
Under-16s Seating: £8.00 in Family Stand
Under-10s Seating: £2.00 (Free in Family Stand)
Note: Discounts are available for tickets bought before the day
of the game and also for home fans in the Family Area

DISABLED INFORMATION

Wheelchairs: Accommodated in front of the new Stand
and the Barking College Stand
Helpers: Admitted
Prices: £12.00 for the disabled. Free of charge for Helpers
Disabled Toilets: Available at the East and West ends of the
ground and also in the Clubhouse
Contact: (020) 8592-7194   (Bookings are necessary)

Travelling Supporters' Information:
Routes: From the North & West: Take the M11 to its end and join the A406 South. At the large roundabout take the slip road
on the left signposted A13 to Dagenham. As you approach Dagenham, stay in the left lane and follow signs for A1306 signposted
Dagenham East. Turn left onto the A1112 at the 5th set of traffic lights by the McDonalds. Proceed along Ballards Road to The
Bull roundabout and bear left. Victoria Road is 450 yards on the left after passing Dagenham East tube station; From the South
& East: Follow signs for the A13 to Dagenham. Take the next slip road off signposted Elm Park & Dagenham East then turn right
at the roundabout. Go straight on at the next roundabout and turn left onto A1306. After ½ mile you will see a McDonalds on
the right. Get into the right hand filter lane and turn right onto A1112. Then as from the North & West.   **SatNav**: RM10 7XL

DOVER ATHLETIC FC

Founded: 1983
Former Names: None
Nickname: 'The Whites'
Ground: Crabble Athletic Ground, Lewisham Road, River, Dover   CT17 0JB
Record Attendance: 5,986 (2015)
Pitch Size: 111 × 73 yards

Colours: White shirts with Black shorts
Telephone N°: (01304) 822373
Fax Number: (01304) 821383
Ground Capacity: 5,652
Seating Capacity: 1,287
Web site: www.doverathletic.com
E-mail: enquiries@doverathletic.com

GENERAL INFORMATION

Car Parking: Street parking
Coach Parking: Street parking
Nearest Railway Station: Kearsney (1 mile)
Nearest Bus Station: Pencester Road, Dover (1½ miles)
Club Shop: At the ground
Opening Times: Saturdays 9.00am to 12.00pm
Telephone N°: (01304) 822373

GROUND INFORMATION

Away Supporters' Entrances & Sections:
Segregation only used when required

ADMISSION INFO (2017/2018 PRICES)

Adult Standing: £17.00
Adult Seating: £18.50
Senior Citizen Standing: £14.00
Senior Citizen Seating: £15.00
Under-18s Standing: £8.00
Under-18s Seating: £9.50
Under-11s Standing/Seating: Free of charge

DISABLED INFORMATION

Wheelchairs: Approximately 6 spaces are available in the Family Stand
Helpers: Please phone the club for information
Prices: Please phone the club for information
Disabled Toilets: Three available
Contact: –   (Bookings are not necessary)

Travelling Supporters' Information:
Routes: Take the A2 to the Whitfield roundabout and take the 4th exit. Travel down the hill to the mini-roundabout then turn left and follow the road for 1 mile to the traffic lights on the hill. Turn sharp right and pass under the railway bridge – the ground is on the left after 300 yards.

EASTLEIGH FC

Founded: 1946
Former Names: Swaythling Athletic FC and Swaythling FC
Nickname: 'The Spitfires'
Ground: The Silverlake Stadium, Stoneham Lane, Eastleigh SO50 9HT
Record Attendance: 3,104 (2006)
Pitch Size: 112 × 74 yards

Colours: Blue shirts with White shorts
Telephone Nº: (023) 8061-3361
Fax Number: (023) 8061-2379
Ground Capacity: 6,000
Seating Capacity: 2,812 (by October 2014)
Web site: www.eastleighfc.com
e-mail: admin@eastleighfc.com

GENERAL INFORMATION

Car Parking: Spaces for 450 cars available (hard standing)
Coach Parking: At the ground
Nearest Railway Station: Southampton Parkway (¾ mile)
Nearest Bus Station: Eastleigh (2 miles)
Club Shop: At the ground
Opening Times: Matchdays and during functions only

GROUND INFORMATION

Away Supporters' Entrances & Sections:
South Stand, entrance via Gates 10 and 11

ADMISSION INFO (2017/2018 PRICES)

Adult Standing: £15.00
Adult Seating: £18.00
Concessionary Standing: £10.00
Concessionary Seating: £12.00
Under-16s Standing/Seating: £4.00 or £7.50
Under-7s Seating: £3.00
Note: Discounted prices are available for advance purchases

DISABLED INFORMATION

Wheelchairs: Accommodated
Helpers: Admitted
Prices: Concessionary prices apply
Disabled Toilets: Available
Contact: (023) 8061-3361   (Bookings are not necessary)

Travelling Supporters' Information:
Routes: Exit the M27 at Junction 5 (signposted for Southampton Airport) and take the A335 (Stoneham Way) towards Southampton. After ½ mile, turn right at the traffic lights into Bassett Green Road. Turn right at the next set of traffic lights into Stoneham Lane and the ground is on the right after ¾ mile.

EBBSFLEET UNITED FC

Founded: 1946	**Colours**: Reds shirts with White shorts
Former Names: Gravesend & Northfleet United FC, Gravesend United FC and Northfleet United FC	**Telephone Nº**: (01474) 533796
	Fax Number: (01474) 324754
Nickname: 'The Fleet'	**Ground Capacity**: 5,258
Ground: Stonebridge Road, Northfleet, Gravesend, Kent DA11 9GN	**Seating Capacity**: 1,220
	Web site: www.ebbsfleetunited.co.uk
Record Attendance: 12,063 (1963)	**E-mail**: info@eufc.co.uk
Pitch Size: 112 × 72 yards	**Note**: The ground is currently under redevelopment

GENERAL INFORMATION

Car Parking: Ebbsfleet International Car Park C (when available) and also street parking
Coach Parking: At the ground
Nearest Railway Station: Northfleet (5 minutes walk)
Nearest Bus Station: Bus Stop outside the ground
Club Shop: At the ground
Opening Times: Matchdays only
Telephone Nº: (01474) 533796

GROUND INFORMATION

Away Supporters' Entrances & Sections:
Only certain games are segregated, when the Swanscombe End turnstiles are allocated to away supporters.
Please contact the club for further details

ADMISSION INFO (2017/2018 PRICES)

Adult Standing: £14.00
Adult Seating: £14.00
Concessionary Standing: £11.00
Concessionary Seating: £11.00
Under-16s Standing/Seating: £6.00
Under-12s Standing/Seating: Free of charge when accompanied by a paying adult (maximum of 2 per adult).

DISABLED INFORMATION

Wheelchairs: 6 spaces are available in the Disabled Area in front of the Main Stand
Helpers: Admitted free of charge
Prices: Please phone the club for information
Disabled Toilets: Available in the Main Stand
Contact: (01474) 533796 (Bookings are necessary)

Travelling Supporters' Information:
Routes: Take the A2 to the Northfleet/Southfleet exit and follow signs for Northfleet (B262). Go straight on at the first roundabout then take the 2nd exit at the 2nd roundabout into Thames Way and follow the football signs for the ground.

FC HALIFAX TOWN

Founded: 1911 (Re-formed 2008)
Former Names: Halifax Town FC
Nickname: 'The Shaymen'
Ground: The MBi Shay Stadium, Shay Syke, Halifax, HX1 2YT
Ground Capacity: 10,568
Seating Capacity: 5,285

Record Attendance: 4,023 (1st January 2011)
Pitch Size: 112 × 73 yards
Colours: Blue shirts and shorts
Telephone Nº: (01422) 341222
Fax Number: (01422) 349487
Web Site: www.fchalifaxtown.co.uk

GENERAL INFORMATION

Car Parking: Adjacent to the East Stand and also Shaw Hill Car Park (Nearby)
Coach Parking: By arrangement with the Club Secretary
Nearest Railway Station: Halifax (10 minutes walk)
Nearest Bus Station: Halifax (15 minutes walk)
Club Shop: At the ground in the East Stand
Opening Times: Please phone for details
Telephone Nº: (01422) 341222 (to change during the 2011/12 season)

GROUND INFORMATION

Away Supporters' Entrances & Sections: Skircoat Stand (Seating only)

ADMISSION INFO (2017/2018 PRICES)

Adult Standing/Seating: £18.00
Under-16s Standing/Seating: £5.00
Senior Citizen Standing/Seating: £15.00
Under-7s Standing/Seating: £3.00

DISABLED INFORMATION

Wheelchairs: 33 spaces available in total in disabled sections in the East Stand and South Stand
Helpers: One admitted free with each paying disabled fan
Prices: Free of charge for the disabled and helpers
Disabled Toilets: Available in the East and South Stands
Contact: (01422) 434212 (Bookings are not necessary)

Travelling Supporters' Information:
Routes: From the North: Take the A629 to Halifax Town Centre. Take the 2nd exit at the roundabout into Broad Street and follow signs for Huddersfield (A629) into Skircoat Road; From the South, East and West: Exit the M62 at Junction 24 and follow Halifax (A629) signs for the Town Centre into Skircoat Road then Shaw Hill for ground. **SatNav**: Use HX1 2YS for the ground.

GATESHEAD FC

Founded: 1930   (Reformed in 1977)
Former Names: Gateshead United FC
Nickname: 'Tynesiders'
Ground: International Stadium, Neilson Road,
Gateshead   NE10 0EF
Record Attendance: 11,750 (1995)
Pitch Size: 110 × 70 yards

Colours: White shirts with Black shorts
Telephone Nº: (0191) 478-3883
Fax Number: (0191) 440-0404
Ground Capacity: 11,750
Seating Capacity: 11,750
Web site: www.gateshead-fc.com
E-mail: info@gateshead-fc.com

GENERAL INFORMATION

Car Parking: At the stadium
Coach Parking: At the stadium
Nearest Railway Station: Gateshead Stadium Metro
(½ mile); Newcastle (British Rail) 1½ miles
Nearest Bus Station: Newcastle Coach Station, St. James'
Boulevard, Newcastle-upon-Tyne, NE1 4BW   (2½ miles)
Club Shop: At the stadium
Opening Times: Matchdays only
Telephone Nº: (0191) 478-3883

GROUND INFORMATION

Away Supporters' Entrances & Sections:
Tyne & Wear County Stand North End or the East Stand

ADMISSION INFO (2017/2018 PRICES)

Adult Seating: £15.00
Senior Citizen/Concessionary Seating: £10.00
Under-16s Seating: £3.00
Under-18s/Student Seating: £8.00
Note: Tickets are cheaper when purchased in advance.

DISABLED INFORMATION

Wheelchairs: 5 spaces available each for home and away
fans by the trackside – Level access with automatic doors
Helpers: Admitted
Prices: Normal prices for the disabled. Helpers are admitted
free of charge.
Disabled Toilets: Available in the Reception Area and on
the 1st floor concourse – accessible by lift.
Contact: (0191) 478-3883   (Bookings are necessary)

Travelling Supporters' Information:
Routes: From the South: Take the A1(M) to Washington Services and fork right onto the A194(M) signposted Tyne Tunnel. At
the next roundabout, turn left onto the A184 signposted for Gateshead. The Stadium is on the right after 3 miles.

GUISELEY AFC

Founded: 1909
Former Names: None
Nickname: 'The Lions'
Ground: Nethermoor Park, Otley Road, Guiseley, Leeds LS20 8BT
Record Attendance: 2,486 (1989/90)
Pitch Size: 110 × 69 yards

Colours: White shirts with Navy Blue shorts
Telephone Nº: 07946 388739
Social Club Phone Nº: (01943) 872872
Fax Number: (01943) 873223
Ground Capacity: 4,000
Seating Capacity: 518
Web site: www.guiseleyafc.co.uk
E-mail: admin@guiseleyafc.co.uk

GENERAL INFORMATION

Car Parking: At the ground and in Netherfield Road – Please do not park in Ings Crescent!
Coach Parking: At the ground
Nearest Railway Station: Guiseley (5 minute walk)
Nearest Bus Station: Bus Stop outside the ground
Club Shop: At the ground
Opening Times: Matchdays only
Telephone Nº: (01943) 879236 (weekdays)
Postal Sales: Yes

GROUND INFORMATION

Away Supporters' Entrances & Sections:
No usual segregation

ADMISSION INFO (2017/2018 PRICES)

Adult Standing: £15.00
Adult Seating: £15.00
Ages 12 to 16 Standing/Seating: £5.00
Under-12s Standing/Seating: Free of charge when accompanied by a paying adult
Concessionary Standing/Seating: £10.00

DISABLED INFORMATION

Wheelchairs: Accommodated by the Players' Entrance
Helpers: Admitted
Prices: Free for both disabled fans and helpers
Disabled Toilets: None
Contact: (01943) 879236 (Bookings are advisable)

Travelling Supporters' Information:
Routes: Exit the M62 at Junction 28 and take the Leeds Ring Road to the roundabout at the junction of the A65 at Horsforth. Turn left onto the A65 and pass through Rawdon to Guiseley keeping Morrison's supermarket on your left. Pass straight through the traffic lights with the Station pub or your right and the ground is on the right after ¼ mile, adjacent to the cricket field.

HARTLEPOOL UNITED FC

Founded: 1908 (**Entered League**: 1921)
Former Names: Hartlepools United FC (1908-68); Hartlepool FC (1968-77)
Nickname: 'The Pool' 'Pools'
Ground: Victoria Park, Clarence Road, Hartlepool, TS24 8BZ
Ground Capacity: 7,865 **Seating Capacity**: 4,249
Record Attendance: 17,426 (15th January 1957)

Pitch Size: 110 × 74 yards
Colours: Blue and White striped shirts with Blue shorts
Telephone Nº: (01429) 272584
Ticket Office: (01429) 272584 Extension 2
Ticket Office e-mail: tickets@hartlepoolunited.co.uk
Fax Number: (01429) 863007
Web Site: www.hartlepoolunited.co.uk
E-mail: enquiries@hartlepoolunited.co.uk

GENERAL INFORMATION

Car Parking: Limited space at the ground (£8.00 charge) and also street parking
Coach Parking: Church Street
Nearest Railway Station: Hartlepool Church Street (5 minutes walk)
Club Shop: At the ground
Opening Times: Please contact the club for details
Telephone Nº: (01429) 260491

GROUND INFORMATION

Away Supporters' Entrances & Sections:
Clarence Road turnstiles 1 & 2 for Smith & Graham Stand

ADMISSION INFO (2017/2018 PRICES)

Adult Standing: £18.00
Adult Seating: £20.00
Child/Senior Citizen Standing: £9.00
Child/Senior Citizen Seating: £10.00
Under-11s: Admitted for £5.00 with a paying adult
Programme Price: £3.00

DISABLED INFORMATION

Wheelchairs: 21 spaces for Home fans in disabled section, Cyril Knowles Stand, 10 spaces for Away fans in the Smith & Graham Stand.
Helpers: One helper admitted per wheelchair
Prices: £20.00 for the Disabled. Helpers free of charge
Disabled Toilets: Available in the Cyril Knowles Stand
Contact: (01429) 272584 (Bookings are advisable)

Travelling Supporters' Information: **Routes**: From the North: Take the A1/A19 to the A179 and follow Town Centre/ Marina signs. Turn right at the roundabout by the 'Historic Quayside' and cross over the Railway bridge. The ground is on the left; From the South & West: Take the A689 following Town Centre/Marina signs. Turn left at the roundabout by the 'Historic Quayside' and cross over the Railway bridge. The ground is on the left.

LEYTON ORIENT FC

Founded: 1881 (**Entered League**: 1905)
Former Names: Glyn Cricket and Football Club
(1881-86); Eagle FC (1886-88); Clapton Orient FC
(1888-1946); Leyton Orient FC (1946-66); Orient FC
(1966-87)
Nickname: 'O's'
Ground: Matchroom Stadium, Brisbane Road,
Leyton, London   E10 5NF

Ground Capacity: 9,285 (all seats)
Record Attendance: 34,345 (21st January 1964)
Pitch Size: 110 × 76 yards
Telephone Nº: 0871 310-1881
Ticket Office: 0871 310-1883
Fax Number: 0871 310-1882
Web Site: www.leytonorient.com
E-mail: info@leytonorient.net

GENERAL INFORMATION
Car Parking: Street parking
Coach Parking: By Police direction
Nearest Railway Station: Leyton Midland Road (½ mile)
Nearest Tube Station: Leyton (Central)
Club Shop: At the ground
Opening Times: Weekdays 9.30am to 4.30pm
Telephone Nº: 0871 310-1889

GROUND INFORMATION
Away Supporters' Entrances & Sections:
East Stand

ADMISSION INFO (2017/2018 PRICES)
Adult Seating: £18.00 – £30.00
Child Seating: £5.00 – free of charge for Under-11s if
booked in advancein the North Family Stand only.
Senior Citizen Seating: £16.00 – £27.00
Note: Tickets are cheaper when purchased in advance
Programme Price: £3.00

DISABLED INFORMATION
Wheelchairs: Spaces are available in the North, East and
West Stands
Helpers: One helper admitted per disabled person
Prices: Free of charge for the disabled and helpers
Disabled Toilets: Available near disabled sections
Contact: 0871 310-1883   (Bookings are necessary)

Travelling Supporters' Information:
Routes: From the North & West: Take A406 North Circular, follow signs for Chelmsford to Edmonton. After 2½ miles take the
3rd exit at the roundabout towards Leyton (A112). Pass the railway station, turn right after ½ mile into Windsor Road and left
into Brisbane Road; From the East: Follow the A12 to London then the City for Leytonstone. Follow Hackney signs into Grove
Road, cross Main Road into Ruckholt Road then turn right into Leyton High Road, turn left after ¼ mile into Buckingham Road
and left into Brisbane Road; From the South: Take the A102M through the Blackwall Tunnel, follow signs for Newmarket (A102)
to join the A11 to Stratford, then follow signs for Stratford Station into Leyton Road to the railway station (then as from North).

MACCLESFIELD TOWN FC

Founded: 1874
Former Names: Macclesfield FC
Nickname: 'The Silkmen'
Ground: Moss Rose Ground, London Road, Macclesfield, Cheshire SK11 7SP
Ground Capacity: 5,977
Seating Capacity: 2,599
Record Attendance: 10,041 (1948)

Pitch Size: 105 × 66 yards
Colours: Blue shirts, White shorts and Blue socks
Telephone Nº: (01625) 264686
Ticket Office: (01625) 264686
Fax Number: (01625) 264692
Web Site: www.mtfc.co.uk
E-mail: office@mtfc.co.uk

GENERAL INFORMATION

Car Parking: Ample parking available near the ground
Coach Parking: Near the ground
Nearest Railway Station: Macclesfield (1 mile)
Nearest Bus Station: Macclesfield
Club Shop: At the ground
Opening Times: Weekdays and matchdays 9.00am to 5.00pm
Telephone Nº: (01625) 264686

GROUND INFORMATION

Away Supporters' Entrances & Sections:
John Askey Terrace and the left side of the Moss Lane Stand

ADMISSION INFO (2017/2018 PRICES)

Adult Standing: £15.00
Adult Seating: £19.00
Concessions Standing: £10.00
Concessions Seating: £15.00
Under-12s Standing: £3.00
Under-12s Seating: £3.00
Under-18s/Student Standing: £5.00
Under-18s/Student Seating: £5.00

DISABLED INFORMATION

Wheelchairs: 45 spaces in front of the Estate Road Stand
Helpers: One helper admitted per disabled fan
Prices: Normal prices apply for the disabled. Helpers are admitted free of charge
Disabled Toilets: 3 available
Contact: (01625) 264686 (Bookings are necessary)

Travelling Supporters' Information:
Routes: From the North: Exit the M6 at Junction 19 to Knutsford, follow the A537 to Macclesfield. Follow signs for the Town Centre, then for the A523 to Leek. The ground is 1 mile out of the Town Centre on the right; From the South: Exit the M6 at Junction 17 for Sandbach and follow the A534 to Congleton. Then take the A536 to Macclesfield. After passing The Rising Sun on the left, turn right into Moss Lane after approximately ¼ mile. Following this lane will take you to the ground.

MAIDENHEAD UNITED FC

Founded: 1870
Former Names: None
Nickname: 'Magpies'
Ground: York Road, Maidenhead, Berks. SL6 1SF
Record Attendance: 7,920 (1936)
Pitch Size: 110 × 75 yards

Colours: Black and White striped shirts, Black shorts
Telephone Nº: (01628) 636314 (Club)
Contact Number: (01628) 636078
Ground Capacity: 4,500
Seating Capacity: 950
Web: www.pitchero.com/clubs/maidenheadunited

GENERAL INFORMATION

Car Parking: Street parking
Coach Parking: Street parking
Nearest Railway Station: Maidenhead (¼ mile)
Nearest Bus Station: Maidenhead
Club Shop: At the ground
Opening Times: Matchdays only
Telephone Nº: (01628) 624739

GROUND INFORMATION

Away Supporters' Entrances & Sections:
No usual segregation

ADMISSION INFO (2017/2018 PRICES)

Adult Standing: £15.00
Adult Seating: £15.00
Concessionary Standing and Seating: £10.00
Under-16s Standing and Seating: £5.00
Note: Junior Magpies (Under-16s) are admitted free to matches in the League.

DISABLED INFORMATION

Wheelchairs: Accommodated
Helpers: Admitted
Prices: Normal prices for the disabled. Free for helpers
Disabled Toilets: Available
Contact: (01628) 636078 (Bookings are not necessary)

Travelling Supporters' Information:
Routes: Exit M4 at Junction 7 and take the A4 to Maidenhead. Cross the River Thames bridge and turn left at the 2nd roundabout passing through the traffic lights. York Road is first right and the ground is approximately 300 yards along on the left.

MAIDSTONE UNITED FC

Founded: 1992 (Reformed)
Former Names: Maidstone Invicta FC
Nickname: 'The Stones'
Ground: Gallagher Stadium, James Whatman Way, Maidstone   ME14 1LQ
Record Attendance: 3,409 (29th April 2017)

Colours: Amber shirts with Black shorts
Telephone Nº: (01622) 753817
Ground Capacity: 4,191
Seating Capacity: 818
Web Site: www.maidstoneunited.co.uk

GENERAL INFORMATION

Car Parking: Various Pay & Display Car Parks available near the ground
Coach Parking: Maidstone coach park (1¼ miles) – please contact the club for further information
Nearest Railway Station: Maidstone East (¼ mile)
Club Shop: Available at the ground
Opening Times: Saturday Matchdays 12.30pm to 5.00pm; Tuesday Matchdays 6.15pm to 9.30pm.
Telephone Nº: (01622) 753817

GROUND INFORMATION

Away Supporters' Entrances & Sections:
No usual segregation – use the main turnstiles unless otherwise advertised.

ADMISSION INFO (2017/2018 PRICES)

Adult Standing: £15.00
Adult Seating: £17.00
Senior Citizen/Student Standing: £12.00
Senior Citizen/Student Seating: £14.00
Ages 11 to 16 Standing: £7.00
Ages 11 to 16 Seating: £9.00
Under-11s Standing: £2.00
Under-11s Seating: £4.00
Programme Price: £3.00

DISABLED INFORMATION

Wheelchairs: Accommodated
Helpers: Admitted
Prices: Normal prices apply for the disabled. Free for helpers
Disabled Toilets: Available
Contact: (01622) 753817   (Bookings are essential)

Travelling Supporters' Information:
Routes: Exit the M20 at Junction 6 or the M2 at Junction 3 and follow the A229 into Maidstone. After entering Maidstone, at the second roundabout (by the White Rabbit pub), take the third exit into James Whatman Way for the stadium. Please check the club web site for details of the nearest car parks.

SOLIHULL MOORS FC

Photo courtesy of Jordan Martin Photography

Founded: 2007
Former Names: Formed by the merger of Solihull Borough FC and Moor Green FC in 2007
Nickname: 'The Moors'
Ground: The Autotmated Technology Group Stadium, Damson Parkway, Solihull   B91 2PP
Record Attendance: 1,912 (vs Birmingham City)
Pitch Size: 114 × 76 yards

Colours: Yellow and Blue hooped shirts, Blue shorts
Telephone Nº: (0121) 705-6770
Fax Number: (0121) 711-4045
Ground Capacity: 3,300
Seating Capacity: 500
Web site: www.solihullmoorsfc.co.uk
E-mail: info@solihullmoorsfc.co.uk

GENERAL INFORMATION
Car Parking: At the ground
Coach Parking: At the ground
Nearest Railway Station: Birmingham International (2 miles)
Nearest Bus Station: Birmingham (5 miles)
Club Shop: At the ground
Opening Times: Matchdays only
Telephone Nº: (0121) 705-6770

GROUND INFORMATION
Away Supporters' Entrances & Sections:
No usual segregation

ADMISSION INFO (2017/2018 PRICES)
Adult Standing: £15.00
Adult Seating: £15.00
Senior Citizen/Junior Standing: £10.00
Senior Citizen/Junior Seating: £10.00
Note: Under-12s are admitted free of charge when accompanied by a paying adult

DISABLED INFORMATION
Wheelchairs: Spaces for 3 wheelchairs are available
Helpers: Admitted
Prices: Normal prices for fans with disabilities. Helpers free
Disabled Toilets: Available
Contact: (0121) 705-6770

Travelling Supporters' Information:
Routes: Exit the M42 at Junction 6 and take the A45 for 2 miles towards Birmingham. Turn left at the traffic lights near the Posthouse Hotel into Damson Parkway (signposted for Landrover/Damsonwood). Continue to the roundabout and come back along the other carriageway to the ground which is situated on the left after about 150 yards.

SUTTON UNITED FC

Founded: 1898
Former Names: Formed by the amalgamation of Sutton Guild Rovers FC and Sutton Association FC
Nickname: 'U's'
Ground: Borough Sports Ground, Gander Green Lane, Sutton, Surrey   SM1 2EY
Record Attendance: 14,000 (1970)

Colours: Amber shirts and shorts
Telephone Nº: (020) 8644-4440
Fax Number: (020) 8644-5120
Ground Capacity: 5,013
Seating Capacity: 765
Web site: www.suttonunited.net

GENERAL INFORMATION

Car Parking: 150 spaces behind the Main Stand
Coach Parking: Space for 1 coach in the car park
Nearest Railway Station: West Sutton (adjacent)
Club Shop: At the ground
Opening Times: Matchdays only
Telephone Nº: (020) 8644-4440

GROUND INFORMATION

Away Supporters' Entrances & Sections:
Collingwood Road entrances and accommodation

ADMISSION INFO (2017/2018 PRICES)

Adult Standing: £15.00
Adult Seating: £17.00
Child Standing: £3.00
Child Seating: £5.00
Senior Citizen Standing: £8.00
Senior Citizen Seating: £10.00

DISABLED INFORMATION

Wheelchairs: 8 spaces are available under cover accommodated on the track perimeter
Helpers: Admitted
Prices: Normal prices apply
Disabled Toilets: Available alongside the Standing Terrace
Contact: (020) 8644-4440   (Bookings are necessary)

Travelling Supporters' Information:
Routes: Exit the M25 at Junction 8 (Reigate Hill) and travel North on the A217 for approximately 8 miles. Cross the A232 then turn right at the traffic lights (past Goose & Granit Public House) into Gander Green Lane. The ground is 300 yards on the left; From London: Gander Green Lane crosses the Sutton bypass 1 mile south of Rose Hill Roundabout. Avoid Sutton Town Centre, especially on Saturdays.

TORQUAY UNITED FC

Founded: 1899
Former Name: Torquay Town FC (1899-1910)
Nickname: 'Gulls'
Ground: Plainmoor Ground, Torquay   TQ1 3PS
Ground Capacity: 6,200   **Seating Capacity**: 2,841
Record Attendance: 21,908 (29th January 1955)
Pitch Size: 112 × 72 yards

Colours: Yellow shirts and Blue shorts
Telephone Nº: (01803) 328666
Ticket Office: (01803) 328666
Fax Number: (01803) 323976
Web Site: www.torquayunited.com
E-mail: reception@torquayunited.com

GENERAL INFORMATION

Car Parking: Street parking
Coach Parking: Lymington Road Coach Station (½ mile)
Nearest Railway Station: Torquay (2 miles)
Nearest Bus Station: Lymington Road (½ mile)
Club Shop: At the ground
Opening Times: Matchdays and during Office Hours
Telephone Nº: (01803) 328666

GROUND INFORMATION

Away Supporters' Entrances & Sections:
Babbacombe End turnstiles for Babbacombe End

ADMISSION INFO (2017/2018 PRICES)

Adult Standing: £15.00
Adult Seating: £17.00 – £19.00
Concessionary Standing: £12.00
Concessionary Seating: £14.00 – £15.00
Under-18s Standing/Seating: £7.00
Note: Family tickets are also available
Programme Price: £3.00

DISABLED INFORMATION

Wheelchairs: 9 spaces in front of Bristow Bench Stand for
home supporters plus 9 spaces in the Away end.
Helpers: One helper admitted per wheelchair
Prices: Normal prices for the disabled. Free for helpers
Disabled Toilets: Available in the Ellacombe End and the
Away End
Contact: (01803) 328666   (Bookings are not necessary)

Travelling Supporters' Information:
Routes: From the North and East: Take the M5 to the A38 then A380 to Torquay. On entering Torquay, turn left at the 1st set of traffic lights after Riviera Way Retail Park into Hele Road. Following signs for the ground, continue straight on over two mini-roundabouts, go up West Hill Road to the traffic lights, then straight ahead into Warbro Road. The ground is situated on the right after 200 yards.

TRANMERE ROVERS FC

Founded: 1884
Former Name: Belmont FC
Nickname: 'Rovers'
Ground: Prenton Park, Prenton Road West, Birkenhead CH42 9PY
Ground Capacity: 16,151 (All seats)
Record Attendance: 24,424 (5th February 1972)

Pitch Size: 110 × 70 yards
Colours: White shirts and shorts
Telephone Nº: 03330 144452
Ticket Office: 03330 144452
Fax Number: (0151) 609-0606
Web Site: www.tranmererovers.co.uk
E-mail: customerservice@tranmererovers.co.uk

GENERAL INFORMATION

Car Parking: Large car park at the ground (£5.00 per car)
Coach Parking: At the ground (£10.00 charge)
Nearest Railway Stations: Hamilton Square, Rock Ferry and Conway Park (approximately 1½ miles)
Nearest Bus Station: Conway Park (Town Centre)
Club Shop: At the ground
Opening Times: Weekdays 9.30am–5.00pm, Matchdays 10.00am–kick-off, non-Saturday matchdays 10.00am–1.00pm
Telephone Nº: 03330 144452

GROUND INFORMATION

Away Supporters' Entrances & Sections:
Cowshed Stand turnstiles 5-9 – access from Borough Road (Away section capacity: 2,500)

ADMISSION INFO (2017/2018 PRICES)

Adult Seating: £19.00 – £22.00
Under-12s Seating: £5.00 – £7.00
Under-17s Seating: £7.00 – £8.00
Senior Citizen Seating: £12.00 – £15.00
Young Persons Ticket (Ages 17-22): £12.00 – £15.00
Programme Price: £3.00
Note: Tickets are available at discounted prices when purchased in advance.

DISABLED INFORMATION

Wheelchairs: 40 spaces in total for Home and Away fans in the disabled section, Bebington Paddock
Helpers: One helper admitted per disabled person
Prices: £12.00
Disabled Toilets: 2 available in the disabled section
Contact: 03330 144452 (Bookings are necessary)

Travelling Supporters' Information:
Routes: From the North: From Liverpool city centre, travel through the Kingsway (Wallasey) Mersey Tunnel (£1.70 toll for cars) then continue onto the M53, exiting at Junction 3. Take the first exit (signposted Birkenhead), continue past Sainsbury's then turn right at the traffic lights by the Halfway House pub then turn left into Prenton Road West at the next set of lights. The ground is on the right after a short distance. From the South: Exit the M53 at Junction 4 and take the 4th exit at the roundabout onto the B5151 Mount Road (the ground is signposted from here). After 2½ miles, turn right at the traffic lights (by the United Reformed Church) into Prenton Road West for the ground.

WOKING FC

Founded: 1889
Former Names: None
Nickname: 'Cardinals'
Ground: Laithwaite Community Stadium, Kingfield, Woking, Surrey GU22 9AA
Record Attendance: 6,000 (1997)
Pitch Size: 109 × 76 yards

Colours: Shirts are Red & White halves, Black shorts
Telephone Nº: (01483) 772470
Daytime Phone Nº: (01483) 772470
Fax Number: (01483) 888423
Ground Capacity: 6,161
Seating Capacity: 2,511
Web site: www.wokingfc.co.uk
E-mail: admin@wokingfc.co.uk

GENERAL INFORMATION

Car Parking: Limited parking at the ground
Coach Parking: Please contact the club for details
Nearest Railway Station: Woking (1 mile)
Nearest Bus Station: Woking
Club Shop: At the ground
Opening Times: Weekdays 10.00am to 3.00pm and Matchdays 1.00pm to 3.00pm.
Telephone Nº: (01483) 772470

GROUND INFORMATION

Away Supporters' Entrances & Sections:
Kingfield Road entrance for the Tennis Club terrace

ADMISSION INFO (2017/2018 PRICES)

Adult Standing: £18.00
Adult Seating: £18.00
Under-16s/Student Standing: £5.00
Under-16s/Student Seating: £5.00
Senior Citizen Standing: £13.00
Senior Citizen Seating: £13.00

DISABLED INFORMATION

Wheelchairs: 8 spaces in the Leslie Gosden Stand and 8 spaces in front of the Family Stand
Helpers: Admitted
Prices: One wheelchair and helper for £13.00
Disabled Toilets: Yes – in the Leslie Gosden Stand and Family Stand area
Contact: (01483) 772470 (Bookings are necessary)

Travelling Supporters' Information:
Routes: Exit the M25 at Junction 10 and follow the A3 towards Guildford. Leave at the next junction onto the B2215 through Ripley and join the A247 to Woking. Alternatively, exit the M25 at Junction 11 and follow the A320 to Woking Town Centre. The ground is on the outskirts of Woking – follow signs on the A320 and A247.

WREXHAM AFC

Founded: 1864
Nickname: 'Red Dragons'
Ground: Racecourse Ground, Mold Road, Wrexham, North Wales   LL11 2AH
Ground Capacity: 10,500 (all seats)
Record Attendance: 34,445 (26th January 1957)
Pitch Size: 111 × 71 yards

Colours: Red shirts with White shorts
Telephone Nº: (01978) 891864
Web Site: www.wrexhamafc.co.uk
E-mail: info@wrexhamfc.tv

GENERAL INFORMATION

Car Parking: Town car parks are nearby and also Glyndwr University (Mold End)
Coach Parking: By Police direction
Nearest Railway Station: Wrexham General (adjacent)
Nearest Bus Station: Wrexham (King Street)
Club Shop: At the ground in the Yale Stand
Opening Times: Monday to Friday 10.00am to 5.00pm
Telephone Nº: (01978) 891864

GROUND INFORMATION

Away Supporters' Entrances & Sections:
Turnstiles 1-4 for the Yale Stand

ADMISSION INFO (2017/2018 PRICES)

Adult Seating: £16.00 – £20.00
Under-16s Seating: £7.00 – £8.00
Under-11s Seating: £1.00 (with a paying adult)
Concessionary Seating: £13.00 – £14.00
Over-80s Seating: £7.00 – £8.00
Note: Discounts apply for advance purchases and Family tickets are also available

DISABLED INFORMATION

Wheelchairs: 35 spaces in the Mold Road Stand
Helpers: One helper admitted per wheelchair
Prices: Normal prices for the disabled. Free for helpers
Disabled Toilets: Available in the disabled section
Contact: (01978) 891864   (Dan Sear)

Travelling Supporters' Information:
Routes: From the North and West: Take the A483 and the Wrexham bypass to the junction with the A541. Branch left at the roundabout and follow Wrexham signs into Mold Road; From the East: Take the A525 or A534 into Wrexham then follow the A541 signs into Mold Road; From the South: Take the the M6, then the M54 and follow the A5 and A483 to the Wrexham bypass and the junction with the A541. Branch right at the roundabout and follow signs for the Town Centre.

THE VANARAMA NATIONAL LEAGUE NORTH

Address

4th Floor, 20 Waterloo Street,
Birmingham   B2 5TB

Phone (0121) 643-3143

Web site   www.footballconference.co.uk

Clubs for the 2017/2018 Season

AFC TELFORD UNITED

Founded: 2004
Former Names: Formed after Telford United FC went out of business. TUFC were previously known as Wellington Town FC
Nickname: 'The Bucks'
Ground: The New Bucks Head Stadium, Watling Street, Wellington, Telford TF1 2TU
Record Attendance: 13,000 (1935)

Pitch Size: 110 × 74 yards
Colours: White shirts and shorts
Telehone N°: (01952) 640064
Fax Number: (01952) 640021
Ground Capacity: 6,300
Seating Capacity: 2,200
Web site: www.telfordunited.com
E-mail: office@telfordutd.co.uk

GENERAL INFORMATION

Car Parking: At the ground (£3.00 charge for cars)
Coach Parking: At the ground
Nearest Railway Station: Wellington
Nearest Bus Station: Wellington
Club Shop: At the ground
Opening Times: Saturday matchdays only from 1.30pm.
Telephone N°: None

GROUND INFORMATION

Away Supporters' Entrances & Sections:
Frank Nagington Stand on the rare occasions when segregation is used

ADMISSION INFO (2017/2018 PRICES)

Adult Standing: £14.00
Adult Seating: £14.00
Under-16s Standing: £3.00
Under-16s Seating: £3.00
Under-20s Standing: £5.00
Under-20s Seating: £5.00
Concessionary Standing: £10.00
Concessionary Seating: £10.00

DISABLED INFORMATION

Wheelchairs: Accommodated at both ends of the ground
Helpers: Admitted
Prices: Normal prices apply
Disabled Toilets: Available by the Sir Stephen Roberts Stand
Contact: (01952) 640064 (Bookings are not necessary)

Travelling Supporters' Information:
Routes: Exit the M54 at Junction 6 and take the A518. Go straight on at the first roundabout, take the second exit at the next roundabout then turn left at the following roundabout. Follow the road round to the right then turn left into the car park.

ALFRETON TOWN FC

Founded: 1959
Former Names: None
Nickname: 'Reds'
Ground: The Impact Arena, North Street, Alfreton, Derbyshire   DE55 7FZ
Record Attendance: 5,023 vs Matlock Town (1960)
Pitch Size: 110 × 75 yards

Colours: Red shirts and shorts
Telephone Nº: (0115) 939-2090
Fax Number: (0115) 949-1846
Ground Capacity: 5,100
Seating Capacity: 1,600
Web site: www.alfretontownfc.com

GENERAL INFORMATION
Car Parking: At the ground
Coach Parking: Available close to the ground
Nearest Railway Station: Alfreton (½ mile)
Nearest Bus Station: Alfreton (5 minutes walk)
Club Shop: At the ground
Opening Times: Matchdays only
Telephone Nº: (01773) 830277

GROUND INFORMATION
Away Supporters' Entrances & Sections:
Segregation is usual so please check prior to the game

ADMISSION INFO (2017/2018 PRICES)
Adult Standing: £14.00
Adult Seating: £14.00
Senior Citizen Standing/Seating: £10.00
Ages 16 to 21 Standing/Seating: £10.00
Under-16s Standing: £2.00 (with a paying adult)
Under-16s Seating: £2.00 (with a paying adult)

DISABLED INFORMATION
Wheelchairs: Accommodated in dedicated areas of the ground
Helpers: Admitted
Prices: Please phone the club for information
Disabled Toilets: Available
Contact: (01773) 830277   (Bookings are not necessary)

Travelling Supporters' Information:
Routes: Exit the M1 at Junction 28 and take the A38 signposted for Derby. After 2 miles take the sliproad onto the B600 then go right at the main road towards the town centre. After ½ mile turn left down North Street and the ground is on the right after 200 yards.

BLYTH SPARTANS FC

Founded: 1899
Former Names: None
Nickname: 'Spartans'
Ground: Croft Park, Blyth, Northumberland, NE24 3JE
Record Attendance: 10,186
Pitch Size: 110 × 70 yards

Colours: Green and White striped shirts, Black shorts
Telephone Nº: (01670) 352373 (Office)
Fax Number: (01670) 545592
Ground Capacity: 4,185
Seating Capacity: 500
Web site: www.blythspartansafc.com

GENERAL INFORMATION

Car Parking: At the ground
Coach Parking: At the ground
Nearest Railway Station: Newcastle
Nearest Bus Station: Blyth (5 minutes walk)
Club Shop: At the ground
Opening Times: Matchdays only
Telephone Nº: c/o (01670) 336379

GROUND INFORMATION

Away Supporters' Entrances & Sections:
No usual segregation

ADMISSION INFO (2017/2018 PRICES)

Adult Standing: £12.00
Adult Seating: £14.00
Concessionary Standing: £6.00
Concessionary Seating: £8.00
Note: Under-10s are admitted free of charge when accompanied by a paying adult
Programme Price: £2.00

DISABLED INFORMATION

Wheelchairs: Accommodated
Helpers: Please phone the club for information
Prices: Please phone the club for information
Disabled Toilets: Yes
Contact: (01670) 352373 (Bookings are necessary)

Travelling Supporters' Information:
Routes: Pass through the Tyne Tunnel and take the left lane for Morpeth (A19/A1). At the 2nd roundabout (after approximately 7 miles) take full right turn for the A189 (signposted Ashington). After 2 miles take the slip road (A1061 signposted Blyth). Follow signs for Blyth turning left at the caravan site. At the 2nd roundabout turn right and the ground is on the left.

BOSTON UNITED FC

Founded: 1933
Former Names: Boston Town FC & Boston Swifts FC
Nickname: 'The Pilgrims'
Ground: Jakemans Stadium, York Street, Boston, PE21 6JN
Ground Capacity: 6,778 **Seating Capacity**: 2,000
Pitch Size: 112 × 72 yards
Record Attendance: 10,086 (1955)

Colours: Amber and Black shirts with Black shorts and Amber socks
Telephone Nº: (01205) 364406 (Office)
Matchday Info: (01205) 364406 or 07860 663299
Fax Number: (01205) 354063
Web Site: www.bufc.co.uk
E-mail: admin@bufc.co.uk

GENERAL INFORMATION

Car Parking: Permit holders only
Coach Parking: Available near to the ground
Nearest Railway Station: Boston (1 mile)
Nearest Bus Station: Boston Coach Station (¼ mile)
Club Shop: In the car park at the ground
Opening Times: Weekdays from 9.00am to 5.00pm and Saturday Matchdays from 11.00am to 5.00pm
Telephone Nº: (01205) 364406

GROUND INFORMATION

Away Supporters' Entrances & Sections:
York Street Entrances 3 & 4 (subject to a move to the Jakemans Stand if so advised by the police)

ADMISSION INFO (2017/2018 PRICES)

Adult Standing: £13.00
Adult Seating: £15.00
Child Standing: £4.00
Child Seating: £5.00
Senior Citizen Standing: £10.00
Senior Citizen Seating: £11.00
Note: Family tickets are also available

DISABLED INFORMATION

Wheelchairs: 7 spaces available for home fans, 4 spaces for away fans below the Main Stand at the Town End
Helpers: One helper admitted per disabled fan
Prices: £13.00 for the disabled. Free of charge for helpers
Disabled Toilets: Available in the Town End Terrace
Contact: (01205) 364406 (Bookings are necessary)

Travelling Supporters' Information:
From the North: Take the A17 from Sleaford, bear right after the railway crossing to the traffic lights over the bridge. Go forward through the traffic lights into York Street for the ground; From the South: Take the A16 from Spalding and turn right at the traffic lights over the bridge. Go forward through the next traffic lights into York Street for the ground.

BRACKLEY TOWN FC

Founded: 1890
Former Names: None
Nickname: 'Saints'
Ground: St. James Park, Churchill Way, Brackley, NN13 7EJ
Record Attendance: 2,604 (2012/13 season)

Colours: Red and Black striped shirts with Black shorts
Telephone Nº: (01280) 704077
Ground Capacity: 3,500
Seating Capacity: 300
Web Site: www.brackleytownfc.com

GENERAL INFORMATION
Car Parking: At the ground (£2.00 charge per car)
Coach Parking: At the ground
Nearest Railway Station: King's Sutton (6¾ miles)
Club Shop: At the ground
Opening Times: Matchdays and by appointment only
Telephone Nº: (01280) 704077

GROUND INFORMATION
Away Supporters' Entrances & Sections:
No usual segregation

ADMISSION INFO (2017/2018 PRICES)
Adult Standing: £12.00
Adult Seating: £12.00
Senior Citizen/Student Standing: £6.00
Senior Citizen/Student Seating: £6.00
Under-18s Standing: £3.00
Under-18s Seating: £3.00
Under-10s Seating/Standing: Free of charge

DISABLED INFORMATION
Wheelchairs: Accommodated
Helpers: Admitted
Prices: Normal prices apply for the disabled. Free for helpers
Disabled Toilets: Available
Contact: (01280) 704077 (Stephen Toghill – bookings are necessary)

Travelling Supporters' Information:
Routes: From the West: Take the A422 to Brackley and take the first exit at the roundabout with the junction of the A43, heading north into Oxford Road. * Go straight on at the next roundabout and continue into Bridge Street before turning right into Churchill Way. The ground is located at the end of the road; From the South: Take the A43 northwards to Brackley. Take the second exit at the roundabout with the junction of the A422 and head into Oxford Road. Then as from * above; From the North-East: Take the A43 to Brackley. Upon reaching Brackley, take the 1st exit at the 1st roundabout, the 2nd exit at the next roundabout then the 3rd exit at the following roundabout into Oxford Road. Then as from * above.

BRADFORD PARK AVENUE FC

Founded: 1907   (Re-formed in 1988)
Former Names: None
Nickname: 'Avenue'
Ground: Horsfall Stadium, Cemetery Road, Bradford, BD6 2NG
Record Attendance: 2,100 (2003)
Pitch Size: 112 × 71 yards

Colours: Green & White hooped shirts, White shorts
Telephone Nº: 07912 271498 (Ground)
Office Address: Hugh House, Foundry Street, Brighouse   HD6 1LT
Office Number: (01484) 400007
Ground Capacity: 3,000   **Seating Capacity**: 1,247
Web site: www.bpafc.com

GENERAL INFORMATION
Car Parking: Street parking and some spaces at the ground
Coach Parking: At the ground
Nearest Railway Station: Bradford Interchange (3 miles)
Nearest Bus Station: Bradford Interchange (3 miles)
Club Shop: At the ground
Opening Times: Matchdays only
Telephone Nº: –

GROUND INFORMATION
Away Supporters' Entrances & Sections:
Segregation only used when required

ADMISSION INFO (2017/2018 PRICES)
Adult Standing/Seating: £10.00
Senior Citizen Standing/Seating: £7.00
Student Standing/Seating: £5.00
Under-18s Standing/Seating: £2.00
Armed Forces Standing/Seating: £5.00 (warrant card must be shown)

DISABLED INFORMATION
Wheelchairs: Accommodated in front of the Stand
Helpers: Please phone the club for information
Prices: Please phone the club for information
Disabled Toilets: Available
Contact: –   (Bookings are not necessary)

Travelling Supporters' Information:
Routes: Exit the M62 at Junction 26 and take the M606 to its end. At the roundabout go along the A6036 (signposted Halifax) and pass Odsal Stadium on the left. At the roundabout by Odsal take the 3rd exit (still A6036 Halifax). After just under 1 mile, turn left at the Kinderhaven Nursery into Cemetery Road. The ground is 150 yards on the left.

CHORLEY FC

Founded: 1883
Former Names: None
Nickname: 'Magpies'
Ground: The Chorley Group Victory Park Stadium, Duke Street, Chorley, PR7 3DU
Record Attendance: 9,679 (1931/32 season)
Pitch Size: 112 × 72 yards

Colours: Black & White striped shirts with Black shorts
Telephone Nº: (01257) 230007
Fax Number: (01257) 275662
Ground Capacity: 4,300
Seating Capacity: 900
Web site: www.chorleyfc.com
E-mail: info@chorleyfc.com

GENERAL INFORMATION

Car Parking: 80 spaces available at the ground (£3.00)
Coach Parking: At the ground
Nearest Railway Station: Chorley (¼ mile)
Nearest Bus Station: 15 minutes from the ground
Club Shop: At the ground
Opening Times: Matchdays only
Telephone Nº: (01257) 230007

GROUND INFORMATION

Away Supporters' Entrances & Sections:
Pilling Lane Stand entrances and accommodation

ADMISSION INFO (2017/2018 PRICES)

Adult Standing: £12.00
Adult Seating: £12.00
Concessionary Standing/Seating: £9.00
Student (Ages 16 to 22) Standing/Seating: £7.00
Under-16s Standing/Seating: £5.00
Under-12s Standing/Seating: Free with a paying adult
Programme Price: £2.50

DISABLED INFORMATION

Wheelchairs: Accommodated by prior arrangement
Helpers: Please contact the club for information
Prices: Please contact the club for information
Disabled Toilets: Available in the Social Club
Contact: (01257) 230007 (Bookings are not necessary)

Travelling Supporters' Information:
Routes: Exit the M61 at Junction 6 and follow the A6 to Chorley. Going past the Yarrow Bridge Hotel on Bolton Road, turn left at the 1st set of traffic lights into Pilling Lane. Take the 1st right into Ashby Street and the ground is the 2nd entrance on the left; Alternative Route: Exit the M6 at Junction 27 and follow signs to Chorley. Turn left at the lights and continue down the A49 for 2½ miles before turning right onto B5251. On entering Chorley, turn right into Duke Street 200 yards past The Plough.

CURZON ASHTON FC

Founded: 1963
Former Names: None
Nickname: 'The Nash'
Ground: Tameside Stadium, Richmond Street, Ashton-under-Lyne   OL7 9HG
Record Attendance: 1,826
Pitch Size: 114 × 72 yards

Colours: Royal Blue shirts and shorts
Telephone Nº: (0161) 330-6033
Fax Number: (0161) 339-8802
Ground Capacity: 4,000
Seating Capacity: 527
Web Site: www.curzon-ashton.co.uk

GENERAL INFORMATION

Car Parking: At the ground
Coach Parking: At the ground
Nearest Railway Station: Ashton-under-Lyne (1 mile)
Club Shop: At the ground
Opening Times: Matchdays only
Telephone Nº: (0161) 330-6033

GROUND INFORMATION

Away Supporters' Entrances & Sections:
No usual segregation

ADMISSION INFO (2017/2018 PRICES)

Adult Standing: £12.00
Adult Seating: £12.00
Concessionary Standing: £6.00
Concessionary Seating: £6.00
Under-16s/Student Standing: £3.00
Under-16s/Student Seating: £3.00
Programme Price: £2.00

DISABLED INFORMATION

Wheelchairs: Accommodated
Helpers: Admitted
Prices: Normal prices apply for the disabled and helpers
Disabled Toilets: Available
Contact: (0161) 330-6033   (Bookings are not necessary)

Travelling Supporters' Information:
Routes: Exit the M60 at Junction 23 and take the A6140 signposted for Ashton. Continue along the A6140 to the set of traffic lights with a Cinema on the right then turn left. Cross over a bridge and go straight across the mini-roundabout before turning left into the ground. NOTE: Diversions may be in force during the 2010/2011 season due to bridge replacement work.

DARLINGTON FC

Founded: 1883 (Re-formed 2012)
Former Names: Successor to the club Darlington FC, formed as Darlington 1883 and renamed in 2017
Nickname: 'Darlo', 'The Quakers'
Ground: Blackwell Meadows, Grange Road, Darlington DL1 5NR
Record Attendance: 3,000 (26th December 2016)
Pitch Size: 110 × 75 yards

Ground Capacity: 3,000
Seating Capacity: 280
Colours: Black and White hooped shirts, Black shorts
Contact Telephone Nº: None
Web Site: www.darlingtonfootballclub.co.uk
E-mail: secretary@darlingtonfc.org

GENERAL INFORMATION

Car Parking: A limited number of spaces at Blackwell Meadows are available on a first-come, first-served basis with a £5.00 fee. Alternatively, use town centre car parks (1½ miles)
Coach Parking: Limited parking at the ground
Nearest Railway Station: Darlington (1½ miles)
Nearest Bus Station: Darlington Town Centre (1½ miles)
Club Shop: At the Dolphin Centre in Darlington
Opening Times: Weekdays 10.00am to 1.00pm.
Telephone Nº: 07488 564642
E-mail: shop@dfc1883.co.uk

GROUND INFORMATION

Away Supporters' Entrances & Sections:
No usual segregation

ADMISSION INFO (2017/2018 PRICES)

Adult Standing: £14.00
Adult Seating: £14.00
Concessionary Standing/Seating: £10.00
Junior Standing/Seating (Ages 5–16): £5.00
Under-5s Standing/Seating: Free of charge
Programme Price: £2.50

DISABLED INFORMATION

Wheelchairs: Accommodated
Helpers: Helpers are admitted
Prices: Normal prices apply for the disabled and helpers
Disabled Toilets: Available
Contact: secretary@darlingtonfc.org (Bookings are necessary)

Travelling Supporters' Information:
Routes: From the South: Exit the A1(M) at Junction 57 and take the A66(M) towards Darlington. At the end of the motorway, continue onto the A66 and take the second exit at the next roundabout onto the A167 Darlington Road. Blackwell Meadows is on the right after 400 yards; From the North: Exit the A1(M) at Junction 59 and take the A167 to Darlington. Upon entering Darlington, continue along the A167, taking the second exit at the roundabout into North Road, the first exit at Northgate Roundabout onto St. Cuthbert's Way then following the road around around Darlington town centre into Victoria Road before turning left at the Baptist church into Grange Road. Blackwell Meadows in on the left after approximately 1 mile.

FC UNITED OF MANCHESTER

Photo courtesy of John Mills @ Altius Photography

Founded: 2005
Nickname: 'F.C.'
Ground: Broadhurst Park, 310 Lightbowne Road, Moston, Manchester M40 0FJ
Ground Capacity: 4,400
Seating Capacity: 750
Pitch Size: 110 × 71 yards

Record Attendance: 4,232 (29th May 2015)
Colours: Red shirts with White shorts
Telephone Nº: (0161) 769-2005
Fax Number: (0161) 769-2014
E-mail: office@fc-utd.co.uk
Web Site: www.fc-utd.co.uk

GENERAL INFORMATION

Car Parking: None available at the ground. A number of car parks are located within ½ mile of Broadhurst Park. Please check the club's web site for further information.
Coach Parking: Phone the club on (0161) 769-2005
Nearest Railway Station: Moston (¾ mile)
Nearest Bus Station: A number of services travel to the ground. Please check the club's web site for further details.
Club Shop: At the ground
Opening Times: Matchdays only
Telephone Nº: (0161) 769-2005

GROUND INFORMATION

Away Supporters' Entrances & Sections:
No usual segregation but away fans will be accommodated in the Lightbowne Road End if necessary.

ADMISSION INFO (2017/2018 PRICES)

Adult Seating: £10.00
Senior Citizen (Over-60s)/Student Seating: £6.00
Under-18s Seating: £3.00
Programme Price: £2.00

DISABLED INFORMATION

Wheelchairs: Spaces for wheelchairs are available in all areas of the ground
Helpers: One helper admitted per wheelchair
Prices: Normal prices for wheelchair users. Helpers are admitted free of charge.
Disabled Toilets: Available behind the Main Stand
Contact: (0161) 769-2005 (Bookings are not necessary)

Travelling Supporters' Information: From the M60 travelling clockwise: Exit the M60 at junction 20 and turn onto the A664. At the traffic signals turn left onto the A6104. Travel straight on and then at the Greengate roundabout take the 4th exit onto Lightbowne Road, the B6393. Carry straight on for around a half a mile and Broadhurst Park is on your left; From the M60 travelling anti-clockwise: Exit the M60 at junction 22, then straight on to Hollingwood Avenue, the A6104. Travel straight on and then at the Greengate roundabout take the 1st exit onto Lightbowne Road, the B6393. Carry straight on for around a half a mile and Broadhurst Park is on your left.

GAINSBOROUGH TRINITY FC

Founded: 1873
Former Names: Trinity Recreationists FC
Nickname: 'The Blues'
Ground: Northolme, Gainsborough, Lincolnshire, DN21 2QW
Record Attendance: 9,760 (1948)
Pitch Size: 111 × 71 yards

Colours: Blue shirts and shorts
Telephone Nº: (01427) 611612
Clubhouse Phone Nº: (01427) 613688
Fax Number: (01427) 613295
Ground Capacity: 4,340
Seating Capacity: 504
Web site: www.gainsboroughtrinity.com

GENERAL INFORMATION
Car Parking: Opposite the ground (£2.00 charge).
Coach Parking: Available by prior arrangement
Nearest Railway Station: Lea Road (2 miles) and also Gainsborough Central on Saturdays only (½ mile)
Nearest Bus Station: Heaton Street (1 mile)
Club Shop: At the ground
Opening Times: Matchdays only
Telephone Nº: (01427) 611612

GROUND INFORMATION
Away Supporters' Entrances & Sections:
No usual segregation

ADMISSION INFO (2017/2018 PRICES)
Adult Standing: £12.00
Adult Seating: £12.00
Concessionary Standing: £8.00
Concessionary Seating: £8.00
Under-16s Standing/Seating: £4.00
Under-5s Standing/Seating: Free of charge

DISABLED INFORMATION
Wheelchairs: Accommodated
Helpers: Please phone the club for information
Prices: Normal prices for the disabled. Free for helpers
Disabled Toilets: Available adjacent to the Main Stand
Contact: (01427) 613295 (Bookings are not necessary)

Travelling Supporters' Information:
Routes: From the North, South and West: Exit the A1 at Blyth services taking the 1st left through to Bawtry. In Bawtry, turn right at the traffic lights onto the A631 straight through to Gainsborough (approx. 11 miles). Go over the bridge to the second set of traffic lights and turn left onto the A159 (Scunthorpe Road). Follow the main road past Tesco on the right through the traffic lights. The ground is situated on right approximately a third of a mile north of the Town Centre; From the East: Take the A631 into Gainsborough and turn right onto the A159. Then as above.

HARROGATE TOWN FC

Founded: 1919
Former Names: Harrogate FC and Harrogate Hotspurs FC
Nickname: 'Town'
Ground: CNG Stadium, Wetherby Road, Harrogate, HG2 7SA
Record Attendance: 4,280 (1950)
Pitch Size: 107 × 72 yards

Colours: Yellow and Black striped shirts, Black shorts
Telephone Nº: (01423) 880675
Club Fax Number: (01423) 883671
Ground Capacity: 3,800
Seating Capacity: 502
Web site: www.harrogatetown.com
E-mail: enquiries@harrogatetown.com

GENERAL INFORMATION

Car Parking: Hospital Car Park adjacent
Coach Parking: At the ground
Nearest Railway Station: Harrogate (¾ mile)
Nearest Bus Station: Harrogate
Club Shop: At the ground
Opening Times: Monday to Friday 9.00am to 3.00pm and also on Matchdays
Telephone Nº: (01423) 885525

GROUND INFORMATION

Away Supporters' Entrances & Sections:
No usual segregation

ADMISSION INFO (2017/2018 PRICES)

Adult Standing: £13.00
Adult Seating: £14.00
Concessionary Standing: £9.00
Concessionary Seating: £10.00
Student Standing/Seating: £3.00
Under-18s Standing: £4.00
Under-18s Seating: £5.00

DISABLED INFORMATION

Wheelchairs: Accommodated at the front of the Main Stand
Helpers: One helper admitted for each disabled fan
Prices: Free of charge for each disabled fan and helper
Disabled Toilets: Available
Contact: (01423) 880675 (Bookings are necessary)

Travelling Supporters' Information:
Routes: From the South: Take the A61 from Leeds and turn right at the roundabout onto the ring road (signposted York). After about 1¼ miles turn left at the next roundabout onto A661 Wetherby Road. The ground is situated ¾ mile on the right; From the West: Take the A59 straight into Wetherby Road from Empress Roundabout and the ground is on the left; From the East & North: Exit the A1(M) at Junction 47, take the A59 to Harrogate then follow the Southern bypass to Wetherby Road for the A661 Roundabout. Turn right towards Harrogate Town Centre and the ground is on the right after ¾ mile.

KIDDERMINSTER HARRIERS FC

Founded: 1886
Nickname: 'Harriers'
Ground: Aggborough, Hoo Road, Kidderminster, Worcestershire   DY10 1NB
Ground Capacity: 6,444
Seating Capacity: 3,143
Record Attendance: 9,155 (1948)

Pitch Size: 110 × 72 yards
Colours: Red and White halved shirts, White shorts
Telephone Nº: (01562) 823931
Fax Number: (01562) 827329
Web Site: www.harriers.co.uk
E-mail: info@harriers.co.uk

GENERAL INFORMATION
Car Parking: At the ground
Coach Parking: As directed
Nearest Railway Station: Kidderminster
Nearest Bus Station: Kidderminster Town Centre
Club Shop: At the ground
Opening Times: Weekdays and First Team Matchdays 9.00am to 5.00pm
Telephone Nº: (01562) 823931

GROUND INFORMATION
Away Supporters' Entrances & Sections:
John Smiths Stand Entrance D and South Terrace Entrance E

ADMISSION INFO (2017/2018 PRICES)
Adult Standing: £14.00
Adult Seating: £16.00
Concessionary Standing: £8.00
Concessionary Seating: £11.00
Under-16s Standing: £1.00
Under-16s Seating: £1.00

DISABLED INFORMATION
Wheelchairs: Home fans accommodated at the front of the Main Stand, Away fans in front of the John Smiths Stand
Helpers: Admitted
Prices: £10.00 for each disabled fan plus one helper
Disabled Toilets: Available by the disabled area
Contact: (01562) 823931   (Bookings are not necessary)

Travelling Supporters' Information:
Routes: Exit the M5 at Junction 3 and follow the A456 to Kidderminster. The ground is situated close by the Severn Valley Railway Station so follow the brown Steam Train signs and turn into Hoo Road about 200 yards downhill of the station. Follow the road along for ¼ mile and the ground is on the left.

LEAMINGTON FC

Founded: 1891
Former Names: Leamington Town FC, Lockheed Borg & Beck FC, AP Leamington FC and Lockheed Leamington FC
Nickname: 'The Brakes'
Ground: The Phillips 66 Community Stadium, Harbury Lane, Leamington Spa   CV33 9QB

Record Attendance: 2,102 (1st May 2017)
Colours: Gold and Black shirts with Black shorts
Telephone Nº: (01926) 430406
Fax Number: (01926) 430406
Ground Capacity: 3,000
Seating Capacity: 250
Web Site: www.leamingtonfc.co.uk

GENERAL INFORMATION

Car Parking: At the ground
Coach Parking: At the ground
Nearest Railway Station: Leamington (4 miles)
Club Shop: Please contact the club for information
Opening Times: Matchdays only
E-mail: shop@leamingtonfc.co.uk

GROUND INFORMATION

Away Supporters' Entrances & Sections:
No usual segregation

ADMISSION INFO (2017/2018 PRICES)

Adult Standing/Seating: £12.00
Concessionary Standing/Seating: £8.00
Under-18s Standing/Seating: £3.00 (Under-12s free)
Student Standing/Seating: £6.00

DISABLED INFORMATION

Wheelchairs: Accommodated
Helpers: Admitted
Prices: Normal prices apply for the disabled. Helpers are admitted free of charge
Disabled Toilets: Available
Contact: (01926) 430406   (Bookings are not necessary)

Travelling Supporters' Information:
Routes: Exit the M40 at Junction 14 and take the A452 towards Leamington continuing at the roundabout into Europa Way (still A452). After approximately ½ mile, take the 4th exit at the roundabout into Harbury Lane (signposted for Harbury and Bishops Tachbrook). Continue on Harbury lane, taking the 3rd exit at the first roundabout and going straight ahead at the traffic lights. The ground is on the left hand side of the road after approximately 1½ miles.   **SatNav**: CV33 9SA

NORTH FERRIBY UNITED FC

Founded: 1934	**Colours**: White shirts with Green trim, Green shorts
Former Names: None	**Telephone Nº**: (01482) 634601
Nickname: 'Villagers' or 'Green & Whites'	**Fax Number**: (01482) 634601
Ground: Eon Visual Media Stadium, Church Road, North Ferriby, East Yorkshire HU14 3AB	**Ground Capacity**: 3,000
	Seating Capacity: 500
Record Attendance: 2,232 (vs Hull City in 2013)	**Web site**: www.northferribyunited.com
Pitch Size: 109 × 76 yards	**E-mail**: info@northferribyunitedfc.co.uk

GENERAL INFORMATION

Car Parking: Limited spaces at the ground
Coach Parking: At the ground
Nearest Railway Station: Ferriby (5 minutes walk)
Nearest Bus Station: Hull
Club Shop: At the ground
Opening Times: Matchdays only
Telephone Nº: (01482) 634601

GROUND INFORMATION

Away Supporters' Entrances & Sections:
No usual segregation

ADMISSION INFO (2017/2018 PRICES)

Adult Standing/Seating: £12.00
Concessionary Standing/Seating: £6.00
Under-16s Standing/Seating: £3.00
Note: Under-12s are admitted free of charge when accompanied by a paying adult (League games only)
Programme Price: £2.00

DISABLED INFORMATION

Wheelchairs: Accommodated
Helpers: Admitted
Prices: Standard prices apply
Disabled Toilets: Available
Contact: (01482) 634601   (Bookings are not necessary)

Travelling Supporters' Information:
Routes: North Ferriby is approximately 8 miles to the west of Hull on the A63. Upon reaching North Ferriby (from the West), proceed through the village past the Duke of Cumberland Hotel and turn right into Church Lane. The ground is situated on the left after half a mile.

NUNEATON TOWN FC

Founded: 1937 (Reformed 2008)
Former Names: Nuneaton Borough FC
Nickname: 'Boro'
Ground: Liberty Way, Attleborough Fields Industrial Estate, Nuneaton CV11 6RR
Record Attendance: 3,111 (2nd May 2009)
Pitch Size: 109 × 74 yards

Colours: Blue shirts and white shorts
Telephone Nº: (024) 7638-5738
Fax Number: (024) 7637-2995
Ground Capacity: 4,614
Seating Capacity: 514
Web site: www.nuneatontownfc.com
E-mail: admin@nuneatontownfc.com

GENERAL INFORMATION

Car Parking: On-site car park plus various other parking spaces available on the nearby Industrial Estate (£2.00 fee)
Coach Parking: At the ground (£10.00 fee)
Nearest Railway Station: Nuneaton (2 miles)
Nearest Bus Station: Nuneaton (2 miles)
Club Shop: Yes – The Boro Shop
Opening Times: By appointment and also on matchdays
Telephone Nº: (024) 7638-5738

GROUND INFORMATION

Away Supporters' Entrances & Sections:
No usual segregation

ADMISSION INFO (2017/2018 PRICES)

Adult Standing: £14.00
Adult Seating: £14.00
Concessionary Standing: £12.00
Concessionary Seating: £12.00
Ages 10 to 17 Standing/Seating: £3.00
Under-10s Standing Seating: Free with a paying adult

DISABLED INFORMATION

Wheelchairs: Accommodated, but only 5 spaces are available
Helpers: Admitted
Prices: Normal prices apply for the disabled and helpers
Disabled Toilets: Available
Contact: (024) 7638-5738 (Bookings are necessary)

Travelling Supporters' Information:
Routes: From the South, West and North-West: Exit the M6 at Junction 3 and follow the A444 into Nuneaton. At the Coton Arches roundabout turn right into Avenue Road which is the A4254 signposted for Hinckley. Continue along the A4254 following the road into Garrett Street then Eastboro Way then turn left into Townsend Drive. Follow the road round before turning left into Liberty Way for the ground; From the North: Exit the M1 at Junction 21 and follow the M69. Exit the M69 at Junction 1 and take the 4th exit at the roundabout onto the A5 (Tamworth, Nuneaton). At Longshoot Junction, turn left onto the A47, continue to the roundabout and take the 1st exit onto A4254 Eastborough Way. Turn right at the next roundabout into Townsend Drive then immediately right again for Liberty Way.

SALFORD CITY FC

Founded: 1940
Former Names: Salford FC, Salford Amateurs FC plus a number of other early names
Nickname: 'The Ammies'
Ground: Moor Lane, Kersal, Salford, Manchester, M7 3PZ
Record Attendance: 3,000 (1980)

Colours: Red shirts with White shorts
Telephone Nº: (0161) 792-6287
Ground Capacity: 3,000
Seating Capacity: 500
Pitch Size: 110 × 70 yards
Web site: www.pitchero.com/clubs/salfordcityfc

GENERAL INFORMATION

Car Parking: Street parking only
Coach Parking: At the ground
Nearest Railway Station: Clifton (2½ miles)
Club Shop: At the ground
Opening Times: Matchdays only
Telephone Nº: ()161) 792-6287

GROUND INFORMATION

Away Supporters' Entrances & Sections:
No usual segregation

ADMISSION INFO (2017/2018 PRICES)

Adult Standing: £10.00
Adult Seating: £10.00
Senior Citizen/Junior Standing: £5.00
Senior Citizen/Junior Seating: £5.00

DISABLED INFORMATION

Wheelchairs: Accommodated
Helpers: Admitted
Prices: Concessionary prices are charged for fans with disabilities. Helpers are admitted free of charge
Disabled Toilets: Available in the club house
Contact: (0161) 792-6287   (Bookings are not necessary)

Travelling Supporters' Information:
Routes: Exit the M60 at Junction 17 and take the A56 Bury New Road towards Prestwich. Continue along, passing the A6044 (Hilton Lane) road then turn right along Moor Lane heading towards Kersal Moor and the Golf Course. The ground is on the left hand side of the road after a few hundred yards.

SOUTHPORT FC

Founded: 1881
Former Names: Southport Vulcan FC, Southport Central FC
Nickname: 'The Sandgrounders' and 'The Port'
Ground: Merseyrail Community Stadium, Haig Avenue, Southport, Merseyside   PR8 6JZ
Record Attendance: 20,010 (1932)
Pitch Size: 110 × 77 yards

Colours: Yellow shirts and shorts
Telephone Nº: (01704) 533422
Fax Number: (01704) 533455
Ground Capacity: 6,008
Seating Capacity: 1,660
Web site: www.southportfc.net

GENERAL INFORMATION

Car Parking: Street parking
Coach Parking: Adjacent to the ground
Nearest Railway Station: Meols Cop (½ mile)
Nearest Bus Station: Southport Town Centre
Club Shop: At the ground
Opening Times: Matchdays from 1.30pm (from 6.30pm on evening matchdays)
Telephone Nº: (01704) 533422

GROUND INFORMATION

Away Supporters' Entrances & Sections:
Blowick End entrances

ADMISSION INFO (2017/2018 PRICES)

Adult Standing: £13.50
Adult Seating: £15.00
Concessionary Standing: £10.00
Concessionary Seating: £11.00
Under-19s Standing/Seating: £5.00
Note: Children aged 11 and under are admitted free of charge when accompanied by a paying adult.

DISABLED INFORMATION

Wheelchairs: Accommodated in front of the Grandstand
Helpers: Admitted
Prices: Concessionary prices charged for the disabled. Helpers are admitted free of charge
Disabled Toilets: Available at the Blowick End of the Grandstand
Contact: (01704) 533422   (Bookings are not necessary)

Travelling Supporters' Information:
Routes: Exit the M58 at Junction 3 and take the A570 to Southport. At the major roundabout (McDonalds/Tesco) go straight on into Scarisbrick New Road, pass over the brook and turn right into Haig Avenue at the traffic lights. The ground is then on the right-hand side.

SPENNYMOOR TOWN FC

Founded: 2005 (Formed by the amalgamation of Evenwood Town and the defunct Spennymoor United)
Former Names: None
Nickname: 'The Moors'
Ground: The Brewery Field, Wood Vue, Spennymoor, Co. Durham   DL16 6JN
Record Attendance: 7,202 (30th March 1957)

Pitch Size: 104 × 65 yards
Colours: Black and White striped shirts, Black shorts
Telephone N°: (01388) 827248
Ground Capacity: 3,000
Seating Capacity: 250
Web Site: www.spennymoortownfc.co.uk

GENERAL INFORMATION

Car Parking: Street parking sometimes available but it can get very congested so fans are recommended to use the car parks behind the Town Hall or Leisure Centre.
Coach Parking: Please contact Steven Lawson on 07871 206474 for information
Nearest Railway Station: Durham (6 miles)
Nearest Bus Station: Durham – the No. 6 bus which stops in Durham Road, Spennymoor (15 minute journey)
Club Shop: At the ground
Opening Times: Matchdays only

GROUND INFORMATION

Away Supporters' Entrances & Sections:
No usual segregation

ADMISSION INFO (2017/2018 PRICES)

Adult Standing/Seating: £12.00
Concessionary Standing/Seating: £8.00
Under-18s Standing/Seating: £3.00
Note: Under-10s are admitted free with a paying adult
Programme Price: £2.50

DISABLED INFORMATION

Wheelchairs: Accommodated by arrangement. Entrance via the Wood Vue turnstiles
Helpers: One helper admitted per wheelchair
Prices: Concessionary prices are charged for fans with disabilities. Helpers are admitted free of charge
Disabled Toilets: Available
Contact: 07871 206474 (Steven Lawson)

Travelling Supporters' Information:
Routes: Exit the A1(M) at Junction 60 and follow the A689 to Rushyford. Take the 3rd exit at the Rushyford roundabout onto the A167 then the 3rd exit at the Chilton roundabout, continuing on the A167 towards Spennymoor. Take the first exit at the Thinford roundabout onto the A688, carry straight on at the small roundabout then take the 3rd exit at the next roundabout into St. Andrew's Lane. Continue along St. Andrew's Lane, turning left at the first roundabout then take the 2nd exit at the mini-roundabout, passing Asda into King Street, and the 2nd exit at the next mini-roundabout into Durham Road. Bear right along Durham Road and Wood Vue is on the left after a short distance.

STOCKPORT COUNTY FC

Photohraph courtesy of Mike Petch – Mphotographic.co.uk

Founded: 1883
Former Names: Heaton Norris Rovers FC
Nickname: 'Hatters' 'County'
Ground: Edgeley Park, Hardcastle Road, Edgeley, Stockport SK3 9DD
Ground Capacity: 10,477 (All seats)
Record Attendance: 27,833 (11th February 1950)
Pitch Size: 111 × 72 yards

Colours: Blue shirts and shorts
Telephone Nº: (0161) 266-2700
Ticket Office: (0161) 266-2700
Web Site: www.stockportcounty.com
E-mail: info@stockportcounty.com

GENERAL INFORMATION

Car Parking: Booth Street (nearby) £4.00
Coach Parking: Booth Street (£20.00)
Nearest Railway Station: Stockport (5 minutes walk)
Nearest Bus Station: Mersey Square (10 minutes walk)
Club Shop: At the ground
Opening Times: Monday to Friday from 12.00pm–4.00pm. Open until 7.45pm on matchdays during the week and also on Saturday matchdays 10.00am – 3.00pm then for 30 minutes after the game.
Telephone Nº: (0161) 266-2700

GROUND INFORMATION

Away Supporters' Entrances & Sections:
Railway End turnstiles for Railway End or turnstiles for Popular Side depending on the opponents

ADMISSION INFO (2017/2018 PRICES)

Adult Seating: £15.00
Concessionary Seating: £10.00
Under-18s Seating: £5.00
Senior Citizen Seating: £10.00
Note: Children under the age of 6 are admitted free.

DISABLED INFORMATION

Wheelchairs: 16 spaces in total. 10 in the Hardcastle Road Stand, 6 in the Cheadle Stand
Helpers: One helper admitted per disabled fan
Prices: £10.00 for the disabled. Helpers free of charge
Disabled Toilets: Yes
Contact: (0161) 266-2700 (Bookings are necessary)

Travelling Supporters' Information:
Routes: From the North, South and West: Exit the M60 at Junction 1 and join the A560, following signs for Cheadle. After ¼ mile turn right into Edgeley Road and after 1 mile turn right into Caroline Street for the ground; From the East: Take the A6 or A560 into Stockport Town Centre and turn left into Greek Street. Take the 2nd exit into Mercian Way (from the roundabout) then turn left into Caroline Street – the ground is straight ahead.

TAMWORTH FC

Founded: 1933
Former Names: None
Nickname: 'The Lambs'
Ground: The Lamb Ground, Kettlebrook, Tamworth, B77 1AA
Record Attendance: 4,920 (3rd April 1948)
Pitch Size: 110 × 73 yards

Colours: Red shirts with Black shorts
Telephone Nº: (01827) 65798
Fax Number: (01827) 62236
Ground Capacity: 4,118
Seating Capacity: 520
Web site: www.thelambs.co.uk

GENERAL INFORMATION

Car Parking: 200 spaces available at the ground – £2.00 per car, £5.00 for per minibus or £10.00 per coach
Coach Parking: At the ground
Nearest Railway Station: Tamworth (½ mile)
Nearest Bus Station: Tamworth (½ mile)
Club Shop: At the ground
Opening Times: Weekdays from 10.00am to 4.00pm and also on Matchdays
Telephone Nº: (01827) 65798 Option 3

GROUND INFORMATION

Away Supporters' Entrances & Sections:
Gates 1 and 2 for Terracing, Gate 2A for seating

ADMISSION INFO (2017/2018 PRICES)

Adult Standing: £12.00
Adult Seating: £14.00
Under-18s Standing: £4.00
Under-18s Seating: £6.00
Under-16s Standing: £2.00 (Under-5s free)
Under-16s Seating: £4.00
Under-5s Seating: £2.00
Concessionary Standing: £7.00
Concessionary Seating: £9.00

DISABLED INFORMATION

Wheelchairs: Accommodated
Helpers: Admitted
Prices: Normal prices apply for Wheelchair disabled. Helpers are charged concessionary rates
Disabled Toilets: Yes
Contact: (01827) 65798 (Bookings are advisable)

Travelling Supporters' Information:
Routes: Exit the M42 at Junction 10 and take the A5/A51 to the town centre following signs for Town Centre/Snowdome. The follow signs for Kettlebrook and the ground is in Kettlebrook Road, 50 yards from the traffic island by the Railway Viaduct and the Snowdome. The ground is signposted from all major roads.

YORK CITY FC

Founded: 1922   (**Re-entered League**: 2012)
Nickname: 'The Minstermen'
Ground: Bootham Crescent, York   YO30 7AQ
Ground Capacity: 8,105
Seating Capacity: 3,509
Record Attendance: 28,123 (5th March 1938)
Pitch Size: 115 × 74 yards

Colours: Red shirts with Blue shorts
Telephone Nº: (01904) 559503
Ticket Office: (01904) 559503 Extension 1
Fax Number: (01904) 631457
Web Site: www.yorkcityfootballclub.co.uk
E-mail: enquiries@yorkcityfootballclub.co.uk

GENERAL INFORMATION

Car Parking: Street parking
Coach Parking: By Police direction
Nearest Railway Station: York (1 mile)
Club Shop: At the ground
Opening Times: Weekdays 12.00am – 5.00pm;
Saturday Matchdays 1.00pm–3.00pm and 4.40pm–5.30pm;
Evening matches open from 6.00pm
Telephone Nº: (01904) 624447 Extension 4

GROUND INFORMATION

Away Supporters' Entrances & Sections:
Grosvenor Road turnstiles for Grosvenor Road End

ADMISSION INFO (2017/2018 PRICES)

Adult Standing: £14.00
Adult Seating: £15.00 – £17.00
Concessionary Standing: £12.00
Concessionary Seating: £10.00 – £12.00
Under-18s Standing/Seating: £6.00   (Under-5s free)
Programme Price: £3.00

DISABLED INFORMATION

Wheelchairs: 18 spaces in total for Home and Away fans in
the disabled section, in front of the Pitchside Bar
Helpers: One helper admitted per disabled person
Prices: £10.00 – £14.00 for fans with disabilities. Helpers
are admitted free of charge
Disabled Toilets: Available at entrance to the disabled area
Contact: (01904) 624447 (Ext. 1) (Bookings not necessary)

Travelling Supporters' Information:
Routes: From the North: Take the A1 then the A59 following signs for York. Cross the railway bridge and turn left after 2 miles
into Water End. Turn right at the end following City Centre signs for nearly ½ mile then turn left into Bootham Crescent; From
the South: Take the A64 and turn left after Buckles Inn onto the Outer Ring Road. Turn right onto the A19, follow City Centre
signs for 1½ miles then turn left into Bootham Crescent; From the East: Take the Outer Ring Road turning left onto the A19.
Then as from the South; From the West: Take the Outer Ring Road turning right onto the A19. Then as from the South.

THE VANARAMA NATIONAL LEAGUE SOUTH

Address

4th Floor, 20 Waterloo Street,
Birmingham   B2 5TB

Phone (0121) 643-3143

Web site   www.footballconference.co.uk

Clubs for the 2017/2018 Season

BATH CITY FC

Founded: 1889
Former Names: Bath AFC, Bath Railway FC and Bath Amateurs FC
Nickname: 'The Romans'
Ground: Twerton Park, Bath   BA2 1DB
Record Attendance: 18,020 (1960)
Pitch Size: 110 × 76 yards

Colours: Black and White striped shirts, Black shorts
Telephone Nº: (01225) 423087
Ground Capacity: 8,840
Seating Capacity: 1,026
Web site: www.bathcityfc.com
E-mail: info@bathcityfootballclub.co.uk

GENERAL INFORMATION

Car Parking: 150 spaces available at the ground
Coach Parking: Available at the ground
Nearest Railway Station: Oldfield Park (1 mile)
Nearest Bus Station: Dorchester Street, Bath
Club Shop: Yes – c/o Club
Opening Times: Matchdays and office hours
Telephone Nº: (01225) 423087

GROUND INFORMATION

Away Supporters' Entrances & Sections:
Turnstiles 17-19

ADMISSION INFO (2017/2018 PRICES)

Adult Standing/Seating: £13.00
Senior Citizen Standing/Seating: £10.00
Students/Under-18s Standing/Seating: £7.00
Under-16s Standing/Seating: £2.00

DISABLED INFORMATION

Wheelchairs: 10 spaces available each for home and away fans in front of the Family Stand
Helpers: Admitted
Prices: Normal prices for the disabled. Free for helpers
Disabled Toilets: Available behind the Family Stand
Contact: (01225) 423087   (Bookings are necessary)

Travelling Supporters' Information:
Route: As a recommendation, avoid exiting the M4 at Junction 18 as the road takes you through Bath City Centre. Instead, exit the M4 at Junction 19 onto the M32. Turn off the M32 at Junction 1 and follow the A4174 Bristol Ring Road south then join the A4 for Bath. On the A4, after passing through Saltford you will reach a roundabout shortly before entering Bath. Take the 2nd exit at this roundabout then follow the road before turning left into Newton Road at the bottom of the steep hill. The ground is then on the right hand side of the road.

BOGNOR REGIS TOWN FC

Founded: 1883
Former Names: None
Nickname: 'The Rocks'
Ground: Nyewood Lane, Bognor Regis   PO21 2TY
Record Attendance: 3,642 (1984)
Pitch Size: 116 × 75 yards

Colours: White shirts with Green trim, Green shorts
Telephone Nº: (01243) 822325
Ground Capacity: 6,000
Seating Capacity: 250
Web site: www.therocks.co.uk

GENERAL INFORMATION
Car Parking: Outside the ground at the Sports Club
Coach Parking: None
Nearest Railway Station: Bognor Regis (1 mile)
Nearest Bus Station: Bognor Regis (1 mile)
Club Shop: At the ground
Opening Times: Matchdays only
Telephone Nº: (01243) 862045

GROUND INFORMATION
Away Supporters' Entrances & Sections:
No usual segregation

ADMISSION INFO (2017/2018 PRICES)
Adult Standing: £12.00
Adult Seating: £13.00
Senior Citizen/Concessionary Standing: £10.00
Senior Citizen/Concessionary Seating: £11.00
Under-18s/Students Standing: £5.00
Under-18s/Students Seating: £5.00
Programme Price: £2.50

DISABLED INFORMATION
Wheelchairs: Accommodated
Helpers: Admitted
Prices: Normal prices apply for fans with disabilities.
Helpers are admitted free of charge
Disabled Toilets: Available
Contact: (01243) 822325   (Bookings are not necessary)

Travelling Supporters' Information:
Routes: From the West: Take the M27/A27 to Chichester then the A259 and pass through Bersted towards Bognor Regis. Turn right into Hawthorne Road then left into Nyewood Lane – the ground is on the right; From the East: Take the A27 from Brighton/Worthing and turn left onto the A29 at Fontwell Roundabout. Travel along Shripney Road and turn right at the second roundabout towards Bersted on the A259 then left into Hawthorne Road – then as above.

BRAINTREE TOWN FC

Founded: 1898
Former Names: Manor Works FC, Crittall Athletic FC, Braintree & Crittall Athletic FC and Braintree FC
Nickname: 'The Iron'
Ground: The Ironmongery Direct Stadium, Clockhouse Way, Braintree, Essex   CM7 3DE
Record Attendance: 4,000 (May 1952)
Pitch Size: 111 × 78 yards

Ground Capacity: 4,222
Seating Capacity: 553
Colours: Orange shirts and socks with Blue shorts
Telephone Nº: (01376) 345617
Fax Number: (01376) 330976
Web site: www.braintreetownfc.org.uk
E-mail: braintreetfc@aol.com

GENERAL INFORMATION
Car Parking: At the ground
Coach Parking: At the ground
Nearest Railway Station: Braintree (1 mile)
Nearest Bus Station: Braintree
Club Shop: At the ground
Opening Times: Matchdays only
Telephone Nº: (01376) 345617

GROUND INFORMATION
Away Supporters' Entrances & Sections:
Gates 7-8

ADMISSION INFO (2017/2018 PRICES)
Adult Standing: £14.00
Adult Seating: £14.00
Concessionary Standing: £10.00
Concessionary Seating: £10.00
Under-18s Standing: £5.00
Under-18s Standing: £5.00

DISABLED INFORMATION
Wheelchairs: Accommodated – 6 spaces available in the Main Stand
Helpers: Admitted
Prices: Normal prices apply for fans with disabilities. Helpers are admitted free of charge
Disabled Toilets: Available
Contact: (01376) 345617

Travelling Supporters' Information:
Routes: Exit the A120 Braintree Bypass at the McDonald's roundabout and follow Cressing Road northwards. The floodlights at the ground are visible on the left ½ mile into town. Turn left into Clockhouse Way then left again for the ground.

CHELMSFORD CITY FC

Founded: 1938
Former Names: Chelmsford FC
Nickname: 'City' or 'Clarets'
Ground: Melbourne Community Stadium, Salerno Way, Chelmsford   CM1 2EH
Record Attendance: 16,807 (at previous ground)
Pitch Size: 109 × 70 yards

Colours: Claret and White shirts and shorts
Telephone Nº: (01245) 290959
Ground Capacity: 3,000
Seating Capacity: 1,400
Web site: www.chelmsfordcityfc.com

GENERAL INFORMATION

Car Parking: Limited space at ground and street parking
Coach Parking: Two spaces available at the ground subject to advance notice
Nearest Railway Station: Chelmsford (2 miles)
Nearest Bus Station: Chelmsford (2 miles)
Club Shop: At the ground
Opening Times: Matchdays only at present
Telephone Nº: (01245) 290959

GROUND INFORMATION

Away Supporters' Entrances & Sections:
No usual segregation

ADMISSION INFO (2017/2018 PRICES)

Adult Standing: £13.00
Adult Seating: £13.00
Under-18s Standing: £5.00
Under-18s Seating: £5.00
Under-12s Standing: Free of charge
Under-12s Seating: Free of charge
Concessionary Standing: £9.00
Concessionary Seating: £9.00

DISABLED INFORMATION

Wheelchairs: Spaces for 11 wheelchairs available
Helpers: Admitted free of charge
Prices: Disabled fans are charged standing admission prices
Disabled Toilets: Available
Contact: (01245) 290959   (Bookings are necessary)

Travelling Supporters' Information:
Route: The ground is situated next to the only set of high rise flats in Chelmsford which can therefore be used as a landmark. From the A12 from London: Exit the A12 at Junction 15 signposted for Chelmsford/Harlow/A414 and head towards Chelmsford along the dual-carriageway. At the third roundabout, immediately after passing the 'Superbowl' on the left, take the first exit into Westway, signposted for the Crematorium and Widford Industrial Estate. Continue along Westway which becomes Waterhouse Lane after the second set of traffic lights. At the next set of lights (at the gyratory system) take the first exit into Rainsford Road, signposted for Sawbridgeworth A1060. Continue along Rainsford Road then turn right into Chignal Road at the second set of traffic lights. Turn right again into Melbourne Avenue and Salerno Way is on the left at the end of the football pitches.

CHIPPENHAM TOWN FC

Founded: 1873
Former Names: None
Nickname: 'The Bluebirds'
Ground: Hardenhuish Park, Bristol Road, Chippenham, Wiltshire   SN14 6LR
Record Attendance: 4,800 (1951)
Pitch Size: 110 × 70 yards

Colours: Royal Blue & White shirts, Royal Blue shorts
Telephone Nº: (01249) 650400
Contact Nº: (01793) 855518
Fax Number: (01249) 650400
Ground Capacity: 3,000
Seating Capacity: 276
Web site: www.pitchero.com/clubs/chippenhamtown

GENERAL INFORMATION

Car Parking: Adjacent to the ground
Coach Parking: At the ground
Nearest Railway Station: Chippenham (1 mile)
Nearest Bus Station: Chippenham
Club Shop: At the ground
Opening Times: Matchdays only
Telephone Nº: –

GROUND INFORMATION

Away Supporters' Entrances & Sections:
No usual segregation

ADMISSION INFO (2017/2018 PRICES)

Adult Standing: £10.00
Adult Seating: £11.00
Concessionary Standing: £6.00
Concessionary Seating: £7.00
Under-18s Standing: £3.00
Under-18s Seating: £4.00
Programme Price: £2.00

DISABLED INFORMATION

Wheelchairs: Accommodated at front of Stand
Helpers: Admitted
Prices: Normal prices apply for the disabled. Free for helpers
Disabled Toilets: None
Contact: (01249) 650400   (Bookings are not necessary)

Travelling Supporters' Information:
Routes: Exit the M4 at Junction 17 and take the A350. Turn right at the first roundabout and follow the road to the junction with the A420. Turn left following 'Town Centre' signs and the ground is just over ½ mile on the left near the Pelican crossing.

CONCORD RANGERS FC

Founded: 1967
Former Names: None
Nickname: 'The Beachboys'
Ground: Aspect Arena, Thames Road, Canvey Island, SS8 0HH
Record Attendance: 1,800

Colours: Yellow shirts with Yellow shorts
Telephone Nº: (01268) 515750
Ground Capacity: 3,000
Seating Capacity: 340
Web Site: www.concordrangers.co.uk

GENERAL INFORMATION
Car Parking: At the ground
Coach Parking: At the ground
Nearest Railway Station: Benfleet
Club Shop: Available via the club's web site shortly
Opening Times: –
Telephone Nº: –

GROUND INFORMATION
Away Supporters' Entrances & Sections:
No usual segregation

ADMISSION INFO (2017/2018 PRICES)
Adult Standing: £12.00
Adult Seating: £12.00
Senior Citizen Standing: £7.00
Senior Citizen Seating: £7.00
Under-16s Standing/Seating: £3.00
Under-10s Standing/Seating: Free of charge

DISABLED INFORMATION
Wheelchairs: Accommodated
Helpers: Admitted
Prices: Normal prices apply for the disabled and helpers
Disabled Toilets: Available
Contact: (01268) 515750   (Bookings are necessary)

Travelling Supporters' Information:
Routes: Take the A13 to the A130 (Canvey Way) for Canvey Island. At the Benfleet roundabout, take the 3rd exit into Canvey Road and continue along through Charfleets Service Road into Long Road. Take the 5th turn on the right into Thorney Bay Road and Thames Road is the 3rd turn on the right. The ground is on the left-hand side around 300 yards down Thames Road.

DARTFORD FC

Founded: 1888
Former Names: None
Nickname: 'The Darts'
Ground: Princes Park Stadium, Grassbanks, Darenth Road, Dartford   DA1 1RT
Record Attendance: 4,097 (11th November 2006)
Pitch Size: 110 × 71 yards

Colours: White Shirts with Black Shorts
Telephone Nº: (01322) 299990
Fax Number: (01322) 299996
Ground Capacity: 4,118
Seating Capacity: 640
Web Site: www.dartfordfc.com
E-mail: info@dartfordfc.com

GENERAL INFORMATION

Car Parking: At the ground
Coach Parking: At the ground
Nearest Railway Station: Dartford (½ mile)
Nearest Bus Station: Dartford (½ mile) & Bluewater (2 miles)
Club Shop: At the ground
Opening Times: Matchdays only – 1.00pm to 6.00pm (but the stadium itself is open daily).
Telephone Nº: (01322) 299990

ADMISSION INFO (2017/2018 PRICES)

Adult Standing: £14.00
Adult Seating: £14.00
Senior Citizen/Concessionary Standing: £7.00
Senior Citizen/Concessionary Seating: £7.00
Youth (Ages 13 to 17) Standing/Seating: £5.00
Junior (Ages 5 to 12) Standing/Seating: £2.00
Under-5s Standing/Seating: Free of charge

DISABLED INFORMATION

Wheelchairs: Accommodated
Helpers: Admitted
Prices: Concessionary prices for the disabled and helpers
Disabled Toilets: Available
Contact: (01322) 299991   (Bookings are not necessary)

Travelling Supporters' Information:
Routes: From M25 Clockwise: Exit the M25 at Junction 1B. At the roundabout, take the 3rd exit onto Princes Road (A225) then the second exit at the next roundabout.* Continue downhill to the traffic lights (with the ground on the left), turn left into Darenth Road then take the 2nd left for the Car Park; From M25 Anti-clockwise: Exit the M25 at Junction 2 and follow the A225 to the roundabout. Take the first exit at this roundabout then the 2nd exit at the next roundabout. Then as from * above.

EASTBOURNE BOROUGH FC

Founded: 1963
Former Names: Langney Sports FC
Nickname: 'The Sports'
Ground: Langney Sports Club, Priory Lane, Langney, Eastbourne BN23 7QH
Record Attendance: 3,770 (5th November 2005)
Pitch Size: 115 × 72 yards

Colours: Red shirts and shorts
Telephone Nº: (01323) 766265
Fax Number: (01323) 741627
Ground Capacity: 4,400
Seating Capacity: 542
Web site: www.ebfc.co.uk

GENERAL INFORMATION

Car Parking: Around 400 spaces available at the ground
Coach Parking: At the ground
Nearest Railway Station: Eastbourne (3 miles)
Nearest Bus Station: Eastbourne   (Service 6A to ground)
Club Shop: At the ground
Opening Times: Matchdays only
Telephone Nº: (01323) 766265

GROUND INFORMATION

Away Supporters' Entrances & Sections:
No usual segregation

ADMISSION INFO (2017/2018 PRICES)

Adult Standing: £13.00
Adult Seating: £13.00
Under-18s Standing: £1.00
Under-18s Seating: £1.00
Senior Citizen Standing: £9.00
Senior Citizen Seating: £9.00

DISABLED INFORMATION

Wheelchairs: 6 spaces available
Helpers: Admitted
Prices: Normal prices apply for fans with disabilities. Free of charge for helpers
Disabled Toilets: Available
Contact: (01323) 766265   (Bookings are necessary)

Travelling Supporters' Information:
Routes: From the North: Exit the A22 onto the Polegate bypass, signposted A27 Eastbourne, Hastings & Bexhill. *Take the 2nd exit at the next roundabout for Stone Cross and Westham (A22) then the first exit at the following roundabout signposted Stone Cross and Westham. Turn right after ½ mile into Friday Street (B2104). At the end of Friday Street, turn left at the double mini-roundabout into Hide Hollow (B2191), passing Eastbourne Crematorium on your right. Turn right at the roundabout into Priory Road, and Priory Lane is about 200 yards down the road on the left; Approaching on the A27 from Brighton: Turn left at the Polegate traffic lights then take 2nd exit at the large roundabout to join the bypass. Then as from *.

EAST THURROCK UNITED FC

Founded: 1969
Former Names: None
Nickname: 'The Rocks'
Ground: FutureFuel Stadium, Rookery Hill, Corringham, Essex, SS17 9LB
Record Attendance: 1,250 (vs Woking, 2003)
Pitch Size: 110 × 72 yards

Colours: Amber shirts with Black shorts
Telephone Nº: (01375) 644166
Ground Capacity: 3,500
Seating Capacity: 250
Web: www.pitchero.com/clubs/eastthurrockunited

GENERAL INFORMATION
Car Parking: At the ground
Coach Parking: At the ground
Nearest Railway Station: Stanford-le-Hope (2 miles)
Nearest Bus Station: Stanford-le-Hope (2 miles)
Club Shop: None
Opening Times: –

GROUND INFORMATION
Away Supporters' Entrances & Sections:
No usual segregation

ADMISSION INFO (2017/2018 PRICES)
Adult Standing: £12.00
Adult Seating: £12.00
Concessionary Standing: £6.00
Concessionary Seating: £6.00
Under-16s Standing: £3.00
Under-16s Seating: £3.00

DISABLED INFORMATION
Wheelchairs: Accommodated
Helpers: Admitted
Prices: Standard prices apply
Disabled Toilets: Available
Contact: 07885 313435 (Bookings are necessary)

Travelling Supporters' Information:
Routes: Exit the M25 at Junction 30 and follow the A13 East. At Stanford-le-Hope turn-off on to the A1014 Coryton, cross over the roundabout and pass through the traffic lights. Then take the first turning on the left signposted Corringham and the ground is immediately on the left.

GLOUCESTER CITY FC |

Gloucester City are groundsharing with Cheltenham Town FC for the 2017/2018 season.

Founded: 1889 (**Re-formed**: 1980)
Forner Names: Gloucester YMCA
Nickname: 'The Tigers'
Ground: Abbey Business Stadium, Whaddon Road,
Cheltenham, Gloucestershire   GL52 5NA
Ground Capacity: 7,136
Seating Capacity: 4,054

Record Attendance: 8,326 (1956)
Pitch Size: 110 × 72 yards
Colours: Yellow and Black Striped shirts, Black shorts
Telephone Nº: 07813 931781
Web Site: www.gloucestercityafc.com
E-mail: contact@gloucestercityafc.com

GENERAL INFORMATION
Car Parking: Available at the ground.
Coach Parking: At the ground
Nearest Railway Station: Cheltenham Spa (2½ miles)
Nearest Bus Station: Cheltenham Royal Well
Club Shop: At the ground
Opening Times: Matchdays only

GROUND INFORMATION
Away Supporters' Entrances & Sections:
No usual segregation

ADMISSION INFO (2017/2018 PRICES)
Adult Standing: £13.00
Adult Seating: £13.00
Under-18s Standing: Free of charge
Under-18s Seating: Free of charge
Concessionary Standing: £7.00
Concessionary Seating: £7.00

DISABLED INFORMATION
Wheelchairs: Accommodated in front of the Stagecoach
West Stand (use main entrance) and in the In 2 Print Stand
Helpers: Admitted free of charge
Prices: Normal prices apply for disabled fans
Disabled Toilets: Available in the In 2 Print Stand, adjacent
to the Stagecoach West Stand and in the Social Club
Contact: 07813 931781

Travelling Supporters' Information:
Routes: The ground is situated to the North-East of Cheltenham, 1 mile from the Town Centre off the B4632 (Prestbury Road)
– Whaddon Road is to the East of the B4632 just North of Pittville Circus. Road signs in the vicinity indicate 'Whaddon Road/
Cheltenham Town FC'.

HAMPTON & RICHMOND BOROUGH FC

Founded: 1921
Former Names: Hampton FC
Nickname: 'Beavers'
Ground: Beveree Stadium, Beaver Close,
off Station Road, Hampton, Middlesex   TW12 2BT
Record Attendance: 3,500 vs West Ham United
Pitch Size: 113 × 71 yards

Colours: Blue shirts with Red flash, Blue shorts
Matchday Phone No: (020) 8979-2456
Fax Number: (020) 8979-2456
Ground Capacity: 3,500
Seating Capacity: 300
Web site: www.hamptonfc.net

GENERAL INFORMATION

Car Parking: At the ground and street parking
Coach Parking: Contact the Club for information
Nearest Railway Station: Hampton
Nearest Bus Station: Hounslow/Kingston/Fulwell
Club Shop: At the ground
Opening Times: Matchdays only
Telephone No: None

GROUND INFORMATION

Away Supporters' Entrances & Sections:
No usual segregation

ADMISSION INFO (2017/2018 PRICES)

Adult Standing: £12.00
Adult Seating: £12.00
Senior Citizen/Concessionary Standing: £7.00
Senior Citizen/Concessionary Seating: £7.00
Under-16s Standing/Seating: £3.00
Note: Under-5s are admitted free of charge
Programme Price: £2.50

DISABLED INFORMATION

Wheelchairs: Accommodated
Helpers: Admitted
Prices: Normal prices apply
Disabled Toilets: Available
Contact: (020) 8979-2456   (Bookings are not necessary)

Travelling Supporters' Information:
Routes: From the South: Exit the M3 at Junction 1 and follow the A308 (signposted Kingston). Turn 1st left after Kempton Park into Percy Road. Turn right at the level crossing into Station Road then left into Beaver Close for the ground; From the North: Take the A305 from Twickenham then turn left onto the A311. Pass through Hampton Hill onto Hampton High Street. Turn right at the White Hart pub (just before the junction with the A308), then right into Station Road and right again into Beaver Close.

HAVANT & WATERLOOVILLE FC

Founded: 1998
Former Names: Formed by the amalgamation of Waterlooville FC and Havant Town FC
Nickname: 'The Hawks'
Ground: Westleigh Park, Martin Road, Havant, PO9 5TH
Record Attendance: 4,400 (2006/07)
Pitch Size: 112 × 76 yards

Colours: White shirts with Blue shorts
Telephone N°: (023) 9278-7822 (Ground)
Fax Number: (023) 9226-2367
Ground Capacity: 6,600
Seating Capacity: 665
Web site: www.havantandwaterloovillefc.co.uk

GENERAL INFORMATION
Car Parking: Space for 300 cars at the ground
Coach Parking: At the ground
Nearest Railway Station: Havant (1 mile)
Nearest Bus Station: Town Centre (1½ miles)
Club Shop: At the ground
Opening Times: Matchdays only
Telephone N°: 07768 271143

GROUND INFORMATION
Away Supporters' Entrances & Sections:
Martin Road End

ADMISSION INFO (2017/2018 PRICES)
Adult Standing: £13.00
Adult Seating: £13.00
Senior Citizen Standing/Seating: £10.00
Concessionary Standing/Seating: £10.00
Note: When accompanied by a paying adult, children under the age of 11 are admitted free of charge

DISABLED INFORMATION
Wheelchairs: 16 spaces available in the Main Stand
Helpers: Admitted
Prices: Normal prices for disabled fans. Free for helpers
Disabled Toilets: Two available
Contact: (023) 9226-7822 (Bookings are necessary)

Travelling Supporters' Information:
Routes: From London or the North take the A27 from Chichester and exit at the B2149 turn-off for Havant. Take the 2nd exit off the dual carriageway into Bartons Road and then the 1st right into Martin Road for the ground; From the West: Take the M27 then the A27 to the Petersfield exit. Then as above.

HEMEL HEMPSTEAD TOWN FC

Founded: 1885
Former Names: Apsley FC and Hemel Hempstead FC
Nickname: 'The Tudors'
Ground: Vauxhall Road, Adeyfield, Hemel Hempstead HP2 4HW
Record Attendance: 2,254 (vs Gosport Borough during the 2013/14 season)

Pitch Size: 112 × 72 yards
Colours: Shirts and Shorts are Red with White trim
Telephone Nº: (01442) 251521
Fax Number: (01442) 264322
Ground Capacity: 3,152
Seating Capacity: 350
Web site: www.hemelfc.com

GENERAL INFORMATION
Car Parking: At the ground
Coach Parking: At the ground
Nearest Railway Station: Hemel Hempstead (1½ miles)
Nearest Bus Station: Hemel Hempstead (¾ mile)
Club Shop: None

GROUND INFORMATION
Away Supporters' Entrances & Sections:
No usual segregation

ADMISSION INFO (2017/2018 PRICES)
Adult Standing: £12.00
Adult Seating: £12.00
Concessionary Standing/Seating: £8.00
Under-18s Standing/Seating: £1.00
Under-5s Standing/Seating: Free of charge
Programme Price: £2.00

DISABLED INFORMATION
Wheelchairs: Accommodated
Helpers: Admitted
Prices: Normal prices apply
Disabled Toilets: Available in the Clubhouse
Contact: (01442) 259777

Travelling Supporters' Information:
Routes: Exit the M1 at Junction 8 and go straight ahead at the first roundabout. When approaching the 2nd roundabout move into the right hand lane and, as you continue straight across be ready to turn right almost immediately through a gap in the central reservation. This turn-off is Leverstock Green Road and continue along this to the double mini-roundabout. At this roundabout turn left into Vauxhall Road and the ground is on the right at the next roundabout.

HUNGERFORD TOWN FC

Founded: 1886
Former Names: Hungerford Swifts FC
Nickname: 'The Crusaders'
Ground: Town Ground, Bulpit Lane, Hungerford, RG17 0AY
Record Attendance: 1,684 (1988/89 season)

Colours: White shirts with Black shorts
Contact Telephone Nº: (01488) 682939
Ground Capacity: 2,500
Seating Capacity: 250
Web: www.pitchero.com/clubs/hungerfordtownfc

GENERAL INFORMATION
Car Parking: At the ground and at the local school
Coach Parking: At the ground
Nearest Railway Station: Hungerford (½ mile)
Club Shop: At the ground
Opening Times: Monday to Friday 6.30pm to 11.00pm and Saturday from 12.00pm to midnight
Telephone Nº: (01488) 682939

GROUND INFORMATION
Away Supporters' Entrances & Sections:
No usual segregation

ADMISSION INFO (2017/2018 PRICES)
Adult Standing: £12.00
Adult Seating: £12.00
Concessionary Standing: £6.00
Concessionary Seating: £6.00
Note: Under-16s are admitted free of charge
Programme Price: £2.00

DISABLED INFORMATION
Wheelchairs: Accommodated
Helpers: Admitted
Prices: £6.00 for the disabled. Free of charge for helpers
Disabled Toilets: Available
Contact: (01488) 682939   (Bookings are not necessary)

Travelling Supporters' Information:
Routes: Exit the M4 at Junction 14 and take the A338 towards Hungerford. Upon reaching Hungerford, turn right at the roundabout onto the A4 Bath Road, turn left at the next rounabout into Charnham Street then turn left again into Bridge Street (A338). The road becomes the High Street and pass under the railway line, carry straight on over three mini-roundabouts then take the next left into Priory Road. Continue to the end of the street and continue left into Priory Road then take the 3rd turning on the left into Bulpit Lane. The entrance to the ground is on the left shortly after crossing the junction with Priory Avenue.

OXFORD CITY FC

Founded: 1882
Former Names: None
Nickname: 'City'
Ground: The Oxford City Community Arena, Marsh Lane, Marston, Oxford OX3 0NQ
Record Attendance: 9,500 (1950)

Colours: Blue & White hooped shirts with Blue shorts
Telephone Nº: (01865) 744493 or 07880 198246
Ground Capacity: 3,218
Seating Capacity: 520
Web Site: www.oxfordcityfc.co.uk
E-mail: ctoxford@btinternet.com

GENERAL INFORMATION
Car Parking: At the ground
Coach Parking: At the ground
Nearest Railway Station: Oxford (3¾ miles)
Club Shop: At the ground
Opening Times: Matchdays only
Telephone Nº: (01865) 744493

GROUND INFORMATION
Away Supporters' Entrances & Sections:
No usual segregation

ADMISSION INFO (2017/2018 PRICES)
Adult Standing: £12.00
Adult Seating: £12.00
Concessionary Standing: £6.00
Concessionary Seating: £6.00
Student Standing: £3.00
Student Seating: £3.00
Under-16s Standing: Free of charge
Under-16s Seating: Free of charge

DISABLED INFORMATION
Wheelchairs: Accommodated
Helpers: Admitted
Prices: Normal prices apply for the disabled and helpers
Disabled Toilets: Available
Contact: (01865) 744493 (Bookings are not necessary)

Travelling Supporters' Information:
Routes: The stadium is located by the side of the A40 Northern Bypass Road next to the Marston flyover junction to the north east of Oxford. Exit the A40 at the Marston junction and head into Marsh Lane (B4150). Take the first turn on the left into the OXSRAD Complex then turn immediately left again to follow the approach road to the stadium in the far corner of the site.

POOLE TOWN FC

Founded: 1880
Former Names: Various names including Poole FC and Poole St. Marys FC
Nickname: 'The Dolphins'
Ground: Tatnam Farm, School Lane, Poole, BH15 3JR
Record Attendance: 1,652 (26/3/2011 at Tatnam)
Pitch Size: 110 × 73 yards

Colours: Red & White halved shirts with Red shorts
Telephone N°: (01794) 517991
Fax N°: (01202) 681167
Office Address: 153 High Street, Poole   BH15 1AU
Ground Capacity: 2,500
Seating Capacity: 268
Web Site: www.pooletownfc.co.uk

GENERAL INFORMATION
Car Parking: At the ground
Coach Parking: At the ground
Nearest Railway Station: Poole (¾ mile)
Nearest Bus Station: Poole
Club Shop: At the ground
Opening Times: Matchdays only
Telephone N°: (01794) 640104

GROUND INFORMATION
Away Supporters' Entrances & Sections:
No usual segregation

ADMISSION INFO (2017/2018 PRICES)
Adult Standing: £12.00
Adult Seating: £12.00
Senior Citizen Standing: £8.00
Senior Citizen Seating: £8.00
Under-18s Standing/Seating: £5.00
Under-13s Standing/Seating: £1.00

DISABLED INFORMATION
Wheelchairs: Accommodated
Helpers: Admitted
Prices: Normal prices apply for the disabled and helpers
Disabled Toilets: One available
Contact: (01794) 681167   (Bookings are not necessary)

Travelling Supporters' Information:
Routes: Take the A35, A3049 or the A349 into Poole to the Fleetsbridge Interchange where these roads all meet. At the interchange, takes the Fleets Lane exit and head southwards into the centre of Poole. Continue along Fleets Lane into Stanley Green Road (passing the Retail Park and part of the Industrial Estate) for approximately ½ mile then turn left into Palmer Road. Take the first turning on the right into School Lane for the ground.

ST. ALBANS CITY FC

Founded: 1908
Former Names: None
Nickname: 'The Saints'
Ground: Clarence Park, York Road, St. Albans, Hertfordshire   AL1 4PL
Record Attendance: 9,757 (27th February 1926)
Pitch Size: 110 × 80 yards

Colours: Blue shirts with Yellow trim, Blue shorts
Telephone Nº: (01727) 848914
Fax Number: (01727) 848914
Ground Capacity: 5,007
Seating Capacity: 667
Web site: www.stalbanscityfc.com

GENERAL INFORMATION
Car Parking: Street parking
Coach Parking: In Clarence Park
Nearest Railway Station: St. Albans City (200 yds)
Club Shop: At the ground
Opening Times: Matchdays only
Telephone Nº: (01727) 864296

GROUND INFORMATION
Away Supporters' Entrances & Sections:
Hatfield Road End when matches are segregated

ADMISSION INFO (2017/2018 PRICES)
Adult Standing/Seating: £15.00
Concessionary Standing/Seating: £10.00
Under-16s Standing/Seating: £5.00
Note: Under-12s are admitted free of charge when accompanied by a paying adult
Programme Price: £2.50

DISABLED INFORMATION
Wheelchairs: Accommodated
Helpers: One admitted per disabled supporter
Prices: Free for disabled, concessionary prices for helpers
Disabled Toilets: Available in the York Road End
Contact: (01727) 864296   (Bookings are not necessary)

Travelling Supporters' Information:
Routes: Take the M1 or M10 to the A405 North Orbital Road and at the roundabout at the start of the M10, go north on the A5183 (Watling Street). Turn right along St. Stephen's Hill and carry along into St. Albans. Continue up Holywell Hill, go through two sets of traffic lights and at the end of St. Peter's Street, take a right turn at the roundabout into Hatfield Road. Follow over the mini-roundabouts and at the second set of traffic lights turn left into Clarence Road and the ground is on the left. Park in Clarence Road and enter the ground via the Park or in York Road and use the entrance by the footbridge.

TRURO CITY FC

Founded: 1889
Former Names: None
Nickname: 'White Tigers'
Ground: Treyew Road, Truro   TR1 2TH
Record Attendance: 2,637 (31st March 2007)
Colours: All Red shirts and shorts

Telephone Nº: (01872) 225400
Fax Number: (01872) 225402
Ground Capacity: 3,200
Seating Capacity: 1,675
Web Site: www.trurocityfc.net

GENERAL INFORMATION
Car Parking: At the ground
Coach Parking: At the ground
Nearest Railway Station: Truro (½ mile)
Club Shop: None

GROUND INFORMATION
Away Supporters' Entrances & Sections:
No usual segregation

ADMISSION INFO (2017/2018 PRICES)
Adult Standing: £13.00
Adult Seating: £13.00
Concessionary Standing: £10.00
Concessionary Seating: £10.00
Under-18s and Students Standing: £5.00
Under-18s and Students Seating: £5.00
Under-12s Standing: Free with a paying adult
Under-12s Seating: Free with a paying adult

DISABLED INFORMATION
Wheelchairs: Accommodated
Helpers: Admitted
Prices: Normal prices apply for the disabled and helpers
Disabled Toilets: Available
Contact: (01872) 225400   (Bookings are not necessary)

Travelling Supporters' Information:
Routes: From the North or East: Take the A30 to the A390 (from the North) or travel straight on the A390 (from the East) to Truro. Continue on the A390 and pass through Truro. The ground is located just to the South West of Truro on the left hand side of the A390 just before the County Hall; From the West: Take the A390 to Truro. The ground is on the right hand side of the road shortly after crossing the railway line and passing the County Hall; From the South: Take the A39 to Truro. At the junction with the A390 turn left onto Green Lane and the ground is on the left hand side of the road after approximately ½ mile.

WEALDSTONE FC

Photo courtesy of Steve Foster/Wealdstone FC

Founded: 1899
Former Names: None
Nickname: 'The Stones' or 'The Royals'
Ground: Grosvenor Vale, Ruislip   HA4 6JQ
Record Attendance: 1,638 (vs Rotherham United)
Colours: Royal Blue shirts with White shorts

Telephone Nº: 07790 038095
Fax Number: (020) 8930-7143
Ground Capacity: 3,607
Seating Capacity: 329
Web site: www.wealdstone-fc.com

GENERAL INFORMATION
Car Parking: 100 spaces available at the ground
Coach Parking: Available outside the ground
Nearest Mainline Station: West Ruislip (1 mile)
Nearest Tube Station: Ruislip (½ mile)
Club Shop: Yes
Opening Times: Orders through the post only
Telephone Nº: –

GROUND INFORMATION
Away Supporters' Entrances & Sections:
No usual segregation

ADMISSION INFO (2017/2018 PRICES)
Adult Standing: £13.00
Adult Seating: £13.00
Concessionary Standing: £9.00
Concessionary Seating: £9.00
Under-18s Standing/Seating: £3.00
Note: Under-14s are admitted free of charge when accompanied by a paying adult

DISABLED INFORMATION
Wheelchairs: Accommodated
Helpers: Admitted
Prices: Normal prices apply
Disabled Toilets: Available
Contact: (01895) 637487

Travelling Supporters' Information:
Routes: Exit the M25 at Junction 16 and take the A40 towards Uxbridge. At the Polish War Memorial Junction with the A4180, follow the Ruislip signs (West End Road). After about 1½ miles, turn right into Grosvenor Vale for the ground.

WELLING UNITED FC

Founded: 1963
Former Names: None
Nickname: 'The Wings'
Ground: Park View Road Ground, Welling, Kent, DA16 1SY
Record Attendance: 4,020 (1989/90)
Pitch Size: 112 × 72 yards

Colours: Shirts are Red with White facings, Red shorts
Telephone Nº: (0208) 301-1196
Daytime Phone Nº: (0208) 301-1196
Fax Number: (0208) 301-5676
Ground Capacity: 4,000
Seating Capacity: 500
Web site: www.wellingunited.com
E-mail: info@wellingunited.com

GENERAL INFORMATION

Car Parking: Street parking only
Coach Parking: Outside of the ground
Nearest Railway Station: Welling (¾ mile)
Nearest Bus Station: Bexleyheath
Club Shop: At the ground
Opening Times: Matchdays only
Telephone Nº: (0208) 301-1196

GROUND INFORMATION

Away Supporters' Entrances & Sections:
Accommodation in the Danson Park End

ADMISSION INFO (2017/2018 PRICES)

Adult Standing: £12.00
Adult Seating: £14.00
Concessionary Standing: £8.00
Concessionary Seating: £10.00
Under-12s Standing: Free with a paying adult
Under-12s Seating: £2.00 with a paying adult

DISABLED INFORMATION

Wheelchairs: Accommodated at the side of the Main Stand
Helpers: Admitted
Prices: Concessionary prices for fans with disabilities. Helpers are admitted free of charge
Disabled Toilets: Yes
Contact: (0208) 301-1196   (Bookings are not necessary)

Travelling Supporters' Information:
Routes: Take the A2 (Rochester Way) from London, then the A221 Northwards (Danson Road) to Bexleyheath. At the end turn left towards Welling along Park View Road and the ground is on the left.

WESTON-SUPER-MARE FC

Founded: 1899
Former Names: Christ Church Old Boys FC
Nickname: 'Seagulls'
Ground: Woodspring Stadium, Winterstoke Road, Weston-super-Mare   BS24 9AA
Record Attendance: 2,623   (vs Woking in F.A. Cup)
Pitch Size: 110 × 70 yards

Colours: White shirts with Black shorts
Telephone N°: (01934) 621618
Fax Number: (01934) 622704
Ground Capacity: 3,071
Seating Capacity: 320
Web site: www.westonsmareafc.co.uk
E-mail: enquiries@wsmafc.co.uk

GENERAL INFORMATION

Car Parking: 140 spaces available at the ground
Coach Parking: At the ground
Nearest Railway Station: Weston-super-Mare (1½ miles)
Nearest Bus Station: Weston-super-Mare (1½ miles)
Club Shop: At the ground
Opening Times: Matchdays only
Telephone N°: (01934) 621618

GROUND INFORMATION

Away Supporters' Entrances & Sections:
No usual segregation

ADMISSION INFO (2017/2018 PRICES)

Adult Standing/Seating: £12.00
Concessionary Standing/Seating: £8.00
Students and Under-16s Standing/Seating: £3.00
Note: Under-8s are admitted free of charge when accompanied by a paying adult or senior citizen.

DISABLED INFORMATION

Wheelchairs: Accommodated in a special disabled section
Helpers: Admitted
Prices: Normal prices apply
Disabled Toilets: Two available
Contact: (01934) 621618   (Bookings are not necessary)

Travelling Supporters' Information:
Routes: Exit the M5 at Junction 21 and follow the dual carriageway (A370) to the 4th roundabout (Asda Winterstoke). Turn left, go over the mini-roundabout and continue for 800 yards. The ground is on the right.

WHITEHAWK FC

Founded: 1945
Former Names: Whitehawk & Manor Farm Old Boys
Nickname: 'The Hawks'
Ground: The Enclosed Ground, East Brighton Park, Wilson Avenue, Brighton BN2 5TS
Record Attendance: 2,100 (1988/89 season)

Colours: Red shirts and shorts
Telephone Nº: (01273) 609736
Ground Capacity: 3,000
Seating Capacity: 200
Web Site: www.whitehawkfc.com

GENERAL INFORMATION
Car Parking: At the ground
Coach Parking: At the ground
Nearest Railway Station: London Road (3¼ miles)
Club Shop: Online sales only
Opening Times: –
Telephone Nº: –

GROUND INFORMATION
Away Supporters' Entrances & Sections:
No usual segregation

ADMISSION INFO (2017/2018 PRICES)
Adult Standing: £12.00
Adult Seating: £12.00
Concessionary Standing: £7.00
Concessionary Seating: £7.00
Ages 12 to 16 Standing/Seating: £3.00
Under-12s Standing/Seating: Free of charge

DISABLED INFORMATION
Wheelchairs: Accommodated
Helpers: Admitted
Prices: Concessionary prices are charged for the disabled and helpers
Disabled Toilets: None
Contact: (01273) 609736   (Bookings are not necessary)

Travelling Supporters' Information:
Routes: Take the M23/A23 to the junction with the A27 on the outskirts of Brighton then follow the A27 towards Lewes. After passing Sussex University on the left, take the slip road onto the B2123 (signposted Falmer, Rottingdean) and continue for approximately 2 miles before turning right at the traffic lights into Warren Road by the Downs Hotel. Continue for approximately 1 mile then turn left at the traffic lights into Wilson Avenue. After 1¼ miles, turn left at the foot of the hill into East Brighton Park.

National League 2016/2017 Season	Aldershot Town	Barrow	Boreham Wood	Braintree Town	Bromley	Chester	Dagenham & Redbridge	Dover Athletic	Eastleigh	Forest Green Rovers	Gateshead	Guiseley	Lincoln City	Macclesfield Town	Maidstone United	North Ferriby United	Solihull Moors	Southport	Sutton United	Torquay United	Tranmere Rovers	Woking	Wrexham	York City
Aldershot Town		2-2	2-0	2-0	4-0	0-0	3-1	1-0	0-1	0-4	3-0	1-0	0-0	1-2	1-0	2-0	2-0	2-1	2-0	1-1	3-1	4-0	2-0	0-0
Barrow	1-0		1-1	2-1	1-1	3-2	2-1	2-3	4-0	2-3	0-0	3-0	3-0	1-1	3-0	3-1	2-1	0-1	0-0	0-0	2-1	2-2	1-1	2-0
Boreham Wood	1-1	1-1		0-1	0-0	1-1	1-3	5-0	0-1	1-0	0-4	0-0	2-0	2-4	0-1	1-0	0-0	2-0	1-0	2-0	0-1	2-1	0-1	1-1
Braintree Town	2-0	0-2	1-2		2-2	1-2	3-2	1-2	1-1	0-1	1-4	2-0	0-4	1-3	0-0	1-0	0-1	2-0	1-0	1-3	0-1	1-3	1-2	1-1
Bromley	2-2	4-1	1-0	0-5		0-1	1-3	0-2	0-5	1-5	3-2	1-1	1-1	0-1	2-0	3-0	0-1	3-1	1-0	1-0	0-2	2-1	4-3	3-0
Chester	2-0	1-2	0-2	1-0	1-1		3-0	5-0	0-1	1-2	1-2	2-0	2-5	2-3	1-3	3-0	0-3	2-2	4-0	1-0	2-3	2-3	1-1	0-2
Dagenham & Redbridge	1-0	1-4	0-2	3-0	2-1	3-2		2-0	4-0	2-1	0-5	1-2	1-0	1-1	0-2	2-0	4-4	3-0	2-2	0-1	0-0	1-1	3-0	1-0
Dover Athletic	1-2	3-1	1-4	6-1	1-0	3-1	1-2		3-0	4-3	2-0	2-0	2-2	1-1	2-0	0-0	3-0	3-1	1-2	1-4	3-1	1-1		2-2
Eastleigh	1-1	2-0	2-2	0-2	2-1	0-3	0-1	2-4		1-1	1-1	2-1	0-1	1-0	3-0	2-0	1-1	2-1	3-0	0-2	0-1	1-1		1-1
Forest Green Rovers	2-1	0-0	2-0	1-1	1-0	2-0	1-1	1-1	1-1		1-0	3-0	2-3	3-0	2-2	0-1	2-1	5-1	1-1	5-5	2-2	4-3	3-0	2-1
Gateshead	1-1	4-1	1-1	1-1	0-2	3-0	1-0	4-2	2-2	3-1		1-1	1-2	1-1	0-0	3-0	1-0	0-0	0-1	2-1	2-2			6-1
Guiseley	1-0	1-0	3-1	0-0	1-4	1-1	0-2	0-4	1-1	0-1	1-1		2-1	1-2	2-1	1-2	1-1	2-1	2-1	1-2	1-1	2-3		6-1
Lincoln City	3-3	1-2	2-0	3-0	1-0	1-0	2-0	2-0	0-0	3-1	3-0	3-1		2-1	2-0	6-1	0-0	4-0	1-3	2-1	2-1	3-2	1-0	1-1
Macclesfield Town	0-2	0-1	0-2	2-0	1-2	0-0	1-4	2-1	0-1	0-1	1-1	1-2	1-2		3-0	1-0	1-3	3-1	0-0	2-0	4-2	3-1	3-0	1-3
Maidstone United	0-2	2-1	1-0	2-1	0-2	4-2	0-1	1-4	2-1	1-4	0-2	1-1	0-0	2-1		1-2	2-4	4-2	1-1	2-1	0-1	0-3	2-2	1-1
North Ferriby United	0-3	0-1	2-4	0-0	1-2	0-1	0-4	1-2	0-3	1-0	3-2	0-0	0-2	0-2			1-4	0-1	2-1	1-0	1-4	2-1	0-0	0-1
Solihull Moors	0-2	2-4	1-1	3-3	1-0	3-2	2-5	2-3	2-0	0-1	0-2	3-2	0-1	2-3	2-0	2-0		4-0	3-0	0-1	0-3	2-2	0-1	1-2
Southport	1-1	1-4	1-0	4-5	1-2	0-1	1-4	0-1	4-3	2-0	0-3	0-1	1-1	1-2	3-2	2-4	0-0		1-1	1-2	1-1	2-1	3-2	2-0
Sutton United	2-0	0-0	1-0	1-2	2-0	5-2	1-0	0-6	1-1	1-2	3-0	1-0	1-1	2-2	2-2	5-1	1-3	2-2		2-0	1-0	4-1	1-0	2-2
Torquay United	0-0	1-1	0-1	3-1	1-0	0-1	1-0	2-1	2-3	4-3	3-1	1-2	1-2	1-1	2-3	2-0	3-0	1-2	2-3		0-0	1-2	1-1	1-1
Tranmere Rovers	2-2	2-0	2-1	1-0	2-2	2-2	0-2	1-0	2-1	0-1	0-1	1-0	0-1	1-0	2-1	1-0	9-0	4-1	3-2	2-1		3-1	2-0	1-0
Woking	1-2	1-1	0-0	2-3	2-1	3-1	1-3	1-0	3-3	0-1	3-0	0-0	1-3	1-0	2-4	1-1	2-1	0-0	2-1	3-1	0-3		2-0	1-1
Wrexham	0-2	2-2	2-1	0-1	2-1	0-0	0-1	0-0	0-0	3-1	0-2	3-1	1-2	0-3	1-3	1-0	1-0	1-0	1-1	1-1	0-1	2-1		2-1
York City	0-1	2-1	1-1	3-0	0-2	1-1	0-2	0-1	3-1	2-2	1-3	1-1	1-4	1-0	1-1	0-1	4-0	5-3	2-2	0-0	0-0	4-1	1-3	

Football Conference National

Season 2016/2017

	P	W	D	L	F	A	Pts
Lincoln City	46	30	9	7	83	40	99
Tranmere Rovers	46	29	8	9	79	39	95
Forest Green Rovers	46	25	11	10	88	56	86
Dagenham & Redbridge	46	26	6	14	79	53	84
Aldershot Town	46	23	13	10	66	37	82
Dover Athletic	46	24	7	15	85	63	79
Barrow	46	20	15	11	72	53	75
Gateshead	46	19	13	14	72	51	70
Macclesfield Town	46	20	8	18	64	57	68
Bromley	46	18	8	20	59	66	62
Boreham Wood	46	15	13	18	49	48	58
Sutton United	46	15	13	18	61	63	58
Wrexham	46	15	13	18	47	61	58
Maidstone United	46	16	10	20	59	75	58
Eastleigh	46	14	15	17	56	63	57
Solihull Moors	46	15	10	21	62	75	55
Torquay United	46	14	11	21	54	61	53
Woking	46	14	11	21	66	80	53
Chester	46	14	10	22	63	71	52
Guiseley	46	13	12	21	50	67	51
York City	46	11	17	18	55	70	50
Braintree Town	46	13	9	24	51	76	48
Southport	46	10	9	27	52	97	39
North Ferriby United	46	12	3	31	32	82	39

Promotion Play-offs

Aldershot Town 0   Tranmere Rovers 3
Dagenham & Redbridge 1   Forest Green Rovers 1

Tranmere Rovers 2   Aldershot Town 2
Tranmere Rovers won 5-2 on aggregate.

Forest Green Rovers 2   Dagenham & Redbridge 0
Forest Green Rovers won 3-1 on aggregate.

Tranmere Rovers 1   Forest Green Rovers 3

Promoted: Lincoln City and Forest Green Rovers

Relegated: York City, Braintree Town, Southport and North Ferriby United

National League North 2016/2017 Season	AFC Fylde	AFC Telford United	Alfreton Town	Altrincham	Boston United	Brackley Town	Bradford Park Avenue	Chorley	Curzon Ashton	Darlington 1883	FC Halifax Town	FC United of Manchester	Gainsborough Trinity	Gloucester City	Harrogate Town	Kidderminster Harriers	Nuneaton Town	Salford City	Stalybridge Celtic	Stockport County	Tamworth	Worcester City
AFC Fylde		1-1	2-0	4-1	9-2	1-1	1-1	0-2	4-1	4-1	3-2	3-1	3-1	2-2	2-1	2-2	2-1	3-3	5-0	0-0	3-1	4-2
AFC Telford United	0-1		1-1	1-0	1-2	0-6	1-3	0-0	3-1	2-0	1-2	1-0	1-0	0-2	0-0	1-0	2-4	0-2	2-0	0-0	1-0	1-0
Alfreton Town	3-5	3-2		3-2	1-0	0-0	0-1	2-2	0-1	0-3	1-0	2-1	4-0	0-2	1-0	3-3	3-3	1-1	0-2	1-1	2-5	0-0
Altrincham	0-6	0-2	1-1		0-1	1-3	2-3	2-2	2-4	2-2	0-1	0-3	2-3	0-1	0-0	1-4	1-3	0-2	0-0	2-3	1-2	2-0
Boston United	0-3	3-0	3-2	0-1		2-3	1-0	3-1	3-1	1-2	1-4	2-3	1-1	2-2	0-3	1-1	1-3	2-0	0-1	0-2	3-0	0-0
Brackley Town	1-3	2-1	2-3	1-1	0-0		2-0	0-1	2-0	2-2	0-0	1-0	0-0	3-0	2-1	2-0	2-1	0-1	5-2	0-3	0-0	0-2
Bradford Park Avenue	1-4	1-1	1-0	2-1	0-2	2-1		0-3	4-4	1-2	1-3	0-0	5-1	0-1	2-3	1-3	1-1	0-2	0-1	0-2	0-0	0-3
Chorley	1-3	2-1	2-1	2-0	2-0	1-1	3-0		0-3	1-1	0-2	3-3	4-0	4-1	1-0	2-1	1-0	0-1	2-1	1-0	1-1	1-0
Curzon Ashton	3-2	1-1	5-0	2-3	4-2	0-0	1-2	1-1		1-2	4-2	1-2	1-2	0-0	1-0	1-6	2-1	0-2	0-0	1-2	1-5	1-1
Darlington 1883	1-1	1-0	3-4	3-1	4-1	1-0	1-0	2-0	1-3		3-2	4-2	5-2	2-0	2-3	0-1	1-2	2-2	4-1	2-1	3-2	5-1
FC Halifax Town	0-1	1-1	1-0	2-2	0-0	1-3	4-0	2-1	3-0	2-2		3-1	2-1	0-1	0-1	2-0	2-0	4-2	1-0	0-0	4-0	3-0
FC United of Manchester	2-3	0-0	4-3	1-1	1-1	1-2	2-3	3-3	0-0	2-3	0-3		5-1	2-4	2-2	1-0	3-0	0-3	2-2	2-0	1-0	1-1
Gainsborough Trinity	1-2	3-1	0-2	2-0	1-2	1-1	1-1	0-2	0-1	3-3	3-2	1-2		1-1	0-2	1-1	2-2	1-0	2-2	0-1	3-2	1-1
Gloucester City	1-5	3-0	4-0	5-0	3-1	1-3	1-0	2-2	0-2	1-2	0-2	2-3	4-1		1-1	1-2	2-2	3-2	2-1	0-1	2-0	3-0
Harrogate Town	3-3	2-1	6-3	2-2	2-0	1-2	1-0	2-1	2-2	1-4	0-3	3-1	1-3	3-1		0-2	3-1	3-3	3-1	1-0	3-4	3-0
Kidderminster Harriers	3-3	1-0	3-0	1-0	1-0	1-2	3-1	0-0	3-2	2-1	1-2	0-2	3-0	3-0	1-0		4-0	1-0	2-1	2-0	6-0	2-1
Nuneaton Town	4-1	1-1	4-1	4-1	2-2	2-2	1-2	1-1	0-1	1-1	2-3	1-4	2-1	1-1	2-1	0-2		0-1	2-1	1-1	1-0	1-1
Salford City	5-0	2-1	4-1	2-1	3-3	1-1	1-1	1-1	1-0	5-1	2-2	1-0	3-2	1-1	0-0	3-0	4-0		1-0	1-1	1-2	3-0
Stalybridge Celtic	2-1	0-2	2-3	0-2	3-3	0-1	4-3	0-1	1-2	0-1	1-0	2-4	3-2	1-3	2-4	1-0	0-4	0-4		1-3	0-4	0-1
Stockport County	1-2	1-1	4-3	3-0	1-1	2-4	1-2	0-0	3-1	3-3	1-1	2-1	1-0	1-1	1-1	0-1	1-1	2-1	3-1		2-1	1-0
Tamworth	1-0	2-1	4-1	2-1	1-0	2-1	5-1	0-1	3-2	2-1	2-6	1-1	1-0	3-1	3-2	3-4	1-2	2-0	2-1	2-2		1-0
Worcester City	1-2	2-1	5-3	3-0	0-2	1-2	0-1	0-1	1-1	2-2	1-2	0-0	2-2	2-3	2-2	0-0	2-3	1-2	4-0	0-0	1-1	

Football Conference North

Season 2016/2017

AFC Fylde	42	26	10	6	109	60	88
Kidderminster Harriers	42	25	7	10	76	41	82
FC Halifax Town	42	24	8	10	81	43	80
Salford City	42	22	11	9	79	44	77
Darlington 1883	42	22	10	10	89	67	76
Chorley	42	20	14	8	60	41	74
Brackley Town	42	20	13	9	66	43	73
Stockport County	42	19	16	7	59	41	73
Tamworth	42	21	6	15	73	67	69
Gloucester City	42	18	10	14	69	61	64
Harrogate Town	42	16	11	15	71	63	59
Nuneaton Town	42	14	13	15	67	69	55
FC United of Manchester	42	14	12	16	69	68	54
Curzon Ashton	42	14	10	18	63	72	52
Boston United	42	12	11	19	54	72	47
Bradford Park Avenue	42	12	7	23	46	74	43
AFC Telford United	42	10	12	20	38	57	42
Alfreton Town	42	11	9	22	62	95	42
Gainsborough Trinity	42	8	12	22	51	84	36
Worcester City	42	7	14	21	44	63	35
Stalybridge Celtic	42	8	5	29	40	89	29
Altrincham	42	4	9	29	39	91	21

Worcester City were relegated, and took a further voluntary demotion to the Midland League for financial reasons.

Promotion Play-offs North

Chorley 0   Kidderminster Harriers 1
Salford City 1   FC Halifax Town 1
Chorley won 2-1 on aggregate.

Kidderminster Harriers 0   Chorley 2
FC Halifax Town 1   Salford City .... 1 (aet)
Aggregate 2-2. FC Halifax Town won 3-0 on penalties.

FC Halifax Town 2   Chorley .... 1 (aet)

Promoted: AFC Fylde and FC Halifax Town

Relegated: Worcester City, Stalybridge Celtic and Altrincham

National League South 2016/2017 Season	Bath City	Bishop's Stortford	Chelmsford City	Concord Rangers	Dartford	Eastbourne Borough	East Thurrock United	Ebbsfleet United	Gosport Borough	Hampton & Richmond Borough	Hemel Hempstead Town	Hungerford Town	Maidenhead United	Margate	Oxford City	Poole Town	St. Albans City	Truro City	Wealdstone	Welling United	Weston-super-Mare	Whitehawk
Bath City		2-0	2-2	2-2	0-1	1-1	2-1	0-1	4-0	1-1	6-0	1-1	1-5	2-0	1-3	3-0	3-0	4-0	1-2	2-1	1-2	2-1
Bishop's Stortford	0-1		1-3	1-0	0-3	1-4	0-4	0-3	0-2	0-1	0-4	1-2	0-2	0-2	0-2	1-4	1-5	4-0	0-3	2-2	2-1	0-3
Chelmsford City	3-1	4-0		4-3	1-1	5-1	2-2	2-1	5-1	2-2	4-4	3-3	0-1	2-0	2-0	3-0	1-1	2-0	4-1	3-1	1-0	1-0
Concord Rangers	0-5	0-0	2-2		1-1	3-1	1-1	0-1	2-2	2-1	2-0	2-4	0-1	0-0	3-3	3-2	3-2	0-2	0-1	0-5	1-3	3-0
Dartford	2-0	4-0	0-1	2-1		4-3	6-1	2-1	0-0	3-1	2-0	2-0	0-0	4-0	1-0	2-1	0-2	5-3	2-2	2-1	3-2	3-1
Eastbourne Borough	1-2	1-0	1-5	2-1	2-3		4-0	0-0	2-0	2-2	3-0	2-2	1-2	2-1	4-0	0-0	3-2	2-0	5-1	7-3	3-4	4-2
East Thurrock United	2-0	2-2	1-2	1-1	1-1	1-1		1-1	5-1	2-1	2-3	0-1	0-0	1-0	2-1	1-2	1-1	5-1	1-1	1-1	5-1	2-3
Ebbsfleet United	1-0	8-0	2-0	4-0	1-0	4-1	6-1		2-0	1-1	2-2	1-0	2-3	4-0	1-0	4-0	3-1	4-2	4-1	5-1	2-1	1-1
Gosport Borough	1-0	0-1	0-6	2-5	0-4	3-1	1-5	1-0		1-1	0-6	1-4	0-2	1-0	0-1	0-2	4-0	3-1	1-3	1-1	1-1	2-3
Hampton & Richmond	2-1	4-1	0-2	1-0	4-1	3-1	1-2	1-1	2-2		3-3	2-0	2-3	1-0	0-1	0-2	4-0	2-2	1-1	3-1	0-2	0-2
Hemel Hempstead Town	3-3	3-2	2-2	2-1	2-2	0-4	1-1	1-1	1-2	1-0		2-0	2-1	3-2	2-0	2-4	2-2	0-1	1-3	2-0	0-5	0-2
Hungerford Town	2-2	2-0	1-1	2-1	2-0	0-2	3-0	1-1	3-3	1-3	3-0		1-1	1-0	2-0	0-1	0-0	5-0	2-0	1-0	2-1	3-1
Maidenhead United	2-1	6-0	1-0	2-0	5-0	2-1	2-1	1-2	3-0	0-0	5-0	2-2		2-0	6-1	1-1	1-1	2-0	2-0	3-0	3-0	2-1
Margate	1-0	0-3	0-2	1-5	0-2	1-1	2-1	0-1	2-0	2-4	2-1	1-1	0-3		0-5	0-2	0-2	2-1	0-1	0-3	3-1	0-2
Oxford City	1-1	3-1	2-0	2-2	1-1	1-0	0-1	1-3	1-2	0-5	1-0	0-6	1-3	1-0		0-1	2-1	1-1	0-3	2-1	0-0	1-0
Poole Town	1-0	1-0	4-0	2-1	2-3	1-1	1-1	0-2	7-0	3-3	1-1	1-1	1-0	1-0	1-3		1-0	2-0	1-1	2-1	2-0	3-1
St. Albans City	1-4	0-1	2-1	2-0	1-0	1-0	2-2	0-3	2-1	2-4	2-2	5-0	2-2	1-1	2-4	4-0		5-0	0-3	3-2	3-0	3-1
Truro City	1-3	1-2	2-2	1-2	0-5	2-2	0-6	1-1	2-0	0-3	2-1	0-3	2-0	3-2	0-0	3-2			1-2	1-1	1-2	4-2
Wealdstone	0-1	5-0	1-1	1-1	0-4	1-4	1-0	2-4	2-1	2-4	1-1	3-0	2-1	2-1	1-1	2-2	2-2	1-2		0-1	1-0	0-0
Welling United	3-1	1-2	0-2	3-1	0-0	3-1	2-0	1-2	4-0	1-2	2-3	0-0	1-2	5-1	4-0	2-1	0-1	3-2	0-1		0-2	1-2
Weston-super-Mare	1-2	5-0	0-0	1-2	1-2	2-0	1-3	0-2	1-1	1-3	3-5	0-1	1-3	3-1	3-0	0-0	0-3	4-2	1-2	2-2		3-1
Whitehawk	0-2	1-0	0-1	0-0	1-0	1-1	2-3	0-3	4-4	1-3	1-4	1-2	1-2	2-0	3-0	2-0	1-1	2-4	0-0	1-0	0-2	

Football Conference South

Season 2016/2017

Maidenhead United	42	30	8	4	93	29	98
Ebbsfleet United	42	29	9	4	96	30	96
Dartford	42	25	9	8	83	45	84
Chelmsford City	42	23	13	6	89	47	82
Poole Town	42	20	11	11	63	49	71
Hungerford Town	42	19	13	10	67	49	70
Hampton & Richmond Borough	42	19	12	11	81	56	69
Wealdstone	42	18	12	12	62	58	66
Bath City	42	18	8	16	71	51	62
St. Albans City	42	16	11	15	72	66	59
Eastbourne Borough	42	16	10	16	82	70	58
Hemel Hempstead Town	42	15	12	15	74	83	57
East Thurrock United	42	14	14	14	73	65	56
Oxford City	42	15	7	20	48	73	52
Weston-super-Mare	42	14	6	22	63	69	48
Welling United	42	12	7	23	64	69	43
Whitehawk	42	12	7	23	51	72	43
Concord Rangers	42	10	12	20	57	75	42
Truro City	42	11	7	24	53	99	40
Gosport Borough	42	9	9	24	45	101	36
Bishop's Stortford	42	8	3	31	29	104	27
Margate	42	7	4	31	26	81	25

Hungerford Town and Poole Town were barred from the play-offs as they did not meet ground size regulations.

Promotion Play-offs South

Hampton & Richmond 1   Ebbsfleet United 2
Chelmsford City 0   Dartford 0

Ebbsfleet United 2   Hampton & Richmond 1
Ebbsfleet United won 4-2 on aggregate.
Darford 1   Chelmsford City 2
Chelmsford City won 2-1 on aggregate

Ebbsfleet United 2   Chelmsford City 1

Promoted: Maidenhead United and Ebbsfleet United

Relegated: Gosport Borough, Bishop's Stortford and Margate

Northern Premier League Premier Division 2016/2017 Season

	Ashton United	Barwell	Blyth Spartans	Buxton	Coalville Town	Corby Town	Frickley Athletic	Grantham Town	Halesowen Town	Hednesford Town	Ilkeston	Marine	Matlock Town	Mickleover Sports	Nantwich Town	Rushall Olympic	Skelmersdale United	Spennymoor Town	Stafford Rangers	Stourbridge	Sutton Coldfield Town	Warrington Town	Whitby Town	Workington
Ashton United	■	0-0	1-1	1-3	3-0	3-1	1-3	4-3	2-1	2-0	1-0	1-4	1-0	3-2	1-1	1-2	1-1	1-2	2-1	0-2	3-1	2-1	3-1	1-2
Barwell	4-1	■	0-2	0-1	1-0	3-0	1-2	1-1	0-0	2-0	2-1	1-2	1-0	2-1	1-1	1-1	4-0	1-1	2-1	0-1	1-1	0-2	1-2	0-2
Blyth Spartans	3-3	2-0	■	0-0	3-1	4-2	5-1	5-1	3-0	5-1	3-1	1-0	4-1	3-0	2-0	2-1	4-0	0-0	2-2	2-1	5-0	0-3	5-1	3-2
Buxton	1-2	0-0	2-2	■	2-1	1-0	2-0	0-1	2-0	2-0	2-0	3-0	2-1	1-0	4-1	3-0	0-0	2-2	1-3	1-1	2-1	3-3	3-0	2-1
Coalville Town	1-3	1-2	0-1	2-1	■	4-1	3-1	1-2	3-1	2-2	0-0	1-4	3-2	3-1	3-3	3-3	0-1	0-0	1-1	1-1	1-2	2-3	2-1	
Corby Town	3-3	0-2	4-3	1-1	1-2	■	2-0	3-0	0-0	3-2	1-2	0-0	0-0	1-0	0-2	1-4	3-0	3-1	0-0	1-2	5-1	0-0	0-2	1-3
Frickley Athletic	1-3	2-3	1-0	4-4	0-4	0-2	■	0-2	0-1	0-1	4-0	2-0	1-0	0-4	1-4	1-0	3-2	0-2	2-1	0-2	2-0	0-3	0-1	2-2
Grantham Town	2-1	2-2	1-2	0-1	5-1	4-0	3-0	■	2-3	4-1	1-1	3-0	0-0	0-4	2-1	1-1	3-3	2-1	2-1	2-1	1-2	2-0	2-2	
Halesowen Town	2-2	1-1	0-5	2-4	1-0	1-1	1-2	1-1	■	1-3	2-1	0-1	0-3	4-2	0-0	1-2	1-0	1-2	2-2	0-1	0-0	1-0	2-0	3-2
Hednesford Town	2-2	1-1	1-2	1-2	1-2	3-0	4-0	1-0	1-2	■	3-1	1-1	0-2	1-0	1-2	2-1	5-0	3-1	0-2	1-1	4-1	1-0	1-1	0-2
Ilkeston	0-2	1-0	0-5	1-0	0-0	0-1	1-0	0-3	0-0	0-2	■	1-2	0-1	0-1	2-3	0-2	3-0	2-3	1-2	1-0	0-2	0-0	0-2	
Marine	3-1	0-0	1-4	5-5	4-2	3-2	3-3	1-1	4-0	3-0	2-2	■	0-1	1-3	1-3	1-1	3-3	1-1	1-0	1-1	1-0	1-4	0-1	
Matlock Town	3-0	2-1	0-0	3-1	0-0	1-2	1-0	2-1	2-1	2-0	0-1	2-1	■	2-2	0-4	2-1	1-1	0-4	3-0	3-1	3-1	1-5	2-1	1-2
Mickleover Sports	4-1	4-1	1-7	0-3	1-2	2-0	2-1	0-1	0-1	7-0	2-1	2-0	0-1	■	0-2	3-1	0-5	1-3	0-4	3-1	1-0	0-1	4-0	
Nantwich Town	3-2	2-2	2-2	1-0	3-0	1-1	3-2	1-1	1-2	1-1	3-0	4-1	0-0	1-3	■	1-0	4-0	1-0	0-1	2-3	1-0	4-1	0-2	0-1
Rushall Olympic	1-1	3-1	0-1	1-0	2-5	0-0	0-1	3-1	1-0	1-1	1-1	2-3	1-2	1-3		■	1-0	1-5	1-0	0-2	3-1	2-2	1-1	1-2
Skelmersdale United	1-10	0-5	1-4	0-6	2-1	1-2	3-1	1-1	1-2	1-3	2-1	0-3	0-2	1-3	2-3	1-2	■	0-2	1-1	0-4	1-3	4-0	0-1	0-1
Spennymoor Town	1-2	2-0	2-1	1-1	5-0	1-0	2-0	1-2	1-1	4-2	3-0	2-1	3-2	3-0	1-1	1-1	7-0	■	1-0	2-2	3-0	4-1	0-1	4-1
Stafford Rangers	1-3	1-1	1-2	1-2	2-1	0-1	2-0	0-1	3-1	1-0	2-0	3-0	0-2	1-1	0-3	0-2	4-4	3-3	■	0-0	0-0	1-2	2-2	0-2
Stourbridge	4-1	2-1	1-2	3-2	2-0	1-0	4-1	1-2	2-2	1-2	3-1	2-0	5-3	0-0	4-2	0-0	2-1	1-1	2-0	■	0-1	0-1	2-1	5-0
Sutton Coldfield Town	2-2	2-1	3-2	1-1	0-3	5-1	3-1	0-2	1-0	0-5	1-0	3-2	2-3	0-1	1-1	0-4	2-0	1-0	1-1	4-1	■	0-1	1-1	1-1
Warrington Town	1-1	1-2	0-2	1-0	2-1	2-1	2-1	1-0	1-0	1-0	4-1	5-3	2-3	2-0	0-2	1-2	2-0	2-1	2-0	2-1		■	0-1	1-2
Whitby Town	2-1	1-2	2-1	4-2	1-1	1-0	4-0	0-2	4-1	1-0	2-1	3-1	1-0	1-1	1-3	1-1	2-1	2-2	1-3	2-0	2-2		■	1-1
Workington	1-0	0-1	0-2	2-0	0-4	1-0	2-0	1-0	1-0	0-2	2-0	4-0	1-3	4-1	3-1	2-0	0-1	3-0	1-2	3-1	0-0	3-1	4-0	■

Evo-Stik League – Northern Premier Division

Season 2016/2017

Team	P	W	D	L	F	A	Pts
Blyth Spartans	46	31	8	7	114	44	101
Spennymoor Town	46	25	12	9	96	48	87
Stourbridge	46	25	10	11	84	51	85
Workington	46	26	5	15	73	56	83
Nantwich Town	46	23	12	11	86	59	81
Whitby Town	46	23	10	13	63	56	79
Buxton	46	22	12	12	81	54	78
Grantham Town	46	22	10	14	75	57	76
Matlock Town	46	22	9	15	68	58	75
Warrington Town	46	22	8	16	64	56	74
Ashton United	46	19	11	16	85	78	68
Rushall Olympic	46	18	10	18	60	60	64
Stafford Rangers	46	16	15	15	63	60	63
Barwell	46	16	14	16	58	53	62
Hednesford Town	46	18	7	21	68	65	61
Mickleover Sports	46	19	3	24	68	71	60
Coalville Town	46	15	10	21	71	79	55
Marine	46	14	13	19	62	74	55
Halesowen Town	46	13	12	21	46	70	51
Sutton Coldfield Town	46	12	11	23	49	79	47
Corby Town	46	12	10	24	49	72	46
Frickley Athletic	46	12	3	31	47	97	39
Ilkeston	46	7	6	33	31	86	27
Skelmersdale United	46	5	9	32	40	118	24

Promotion Play-offs

Spennymoor Town 2   Nantwich Town 0
Stourbridge 3   Workington .... 2 (aet)

Spennymoor Town 1   Stourbridge 0

Promoted: Blyth Spartans and Spennymoor Town

Relegated: Corby Town, Frickley Athletic, Ilkeston and Skelmersdale United

Southern Football League — Premier Division — 2016/2017 Season

	Banbury United	Basingstoke Town	Biggleswade Town	Cambridge City	Chesham United	Chippenham Town	Cinderford Town	Cirencester Town	Dorchester Town	Dunstable Town	Frome Town	Hayes & Yeading United	Hitchin Town	Kettering Town	King's Lynn Town	Kings Langley	Leamington	Merthyr Town	Redditch United	Slough Town	St. Ives Town	St. Neots Town	Stratford Town	Weymouth
Banbury United		0-1	1-1	2-0	1-0	2-1	4-0	2-1	1-2	0-1	1-2	5-0	1-1	1-2	4-0	3-0	1-0	1-1	0-1	1-0	1-0	2-1	2-1	1-1
Basingstoke Town	0-1		2-1	2-1	3-2	1-2	3-0	0-1	1-1	5-1	1-3	1-1	1-1	3-0	1-2	3-0	0-2	3-2	0-1	4-1	0-2	1-0	2-1	1-6
Biggleswade Town	2-1	0-0		2-1	2-2	2-2	5-0	6-0	3-0	2-2	4-1	6-0	1-3	2-2	2-0	0-4	2-0	2-5	2-0	3-0	3-1	2-0	1-2	1-3
Cambridge City	1-2	0-2	1-1		3-1	1-3	1-0	2-1	1-0	0-2	0-3	2-2	0-4	2-3	0-0	1-1	1-1	1-0	1-4	3-4	1-2	3-0	0-0	2-1
Chesham United	0-4	4-0	1-2	3-1		1-3	1-0	3-0	3-0	1-0	1-1	6-0	2-0	1-0	1-2	5-2	0-1	1-1	1-1	1-1	2-0	3-2	1-1	1-1
Chippenham Town	0-1	2-0	2-0	5-0	3-1		1-0	4-1	4-0	1-0	2-2	3-0	1-0	2-1	1-1	1-0	3-1	1-1	3-3	2-0	1-2	2-1	2-1	2-0
Cinderford Town	1-2	2-3	1-2	0-1	0-1	3-2		0-2	4-0	1-3	4-2	1-2	0-4	1-2	0-4	2-1	1-2	2-1	2-1	0-1	5-2	2-1	1-2	2-2
Cirencester Town	1-4	2-3	1-0	0-3	1-2	3-3	3-2		4-1	2-0	1-4	1-2	0-0	1-6	1-1	0-1	1-0	0-2	2-1	1-3	1-2	2-1	1-2	3-0
Dorchester Town	0-1	1-1	2-1	0-2	3-2	1-3	2-0	2-2		2-0	3-0	2-1	2-2	0-2	1-1	1-0	2-2	1-2	0-0	0-4	1-1	1-0	2-2	1-1
Dunstable Town	1-0	1-3	0-2	2-1	0-0	1-2	2-0	1-1	2-1		0-2	0-2	2-3	0-0	1-2	0-2	0-1	1-0	0-1	4-1	1-0	2-0	1-1	1-1
Frome Town	1-2	1-1	2-0	2-0	2-0	0-1	3-2	3-2	0-4	1-0		2-1	1-3	3-3	1-3	0-0	1-0	2-2	8-1	1-0	2-2	1-1	3-1	2-0
Hayes & Yeading United	0-1	2-3	0-0	0-0	1-0	1-2	5-0	1-1	1-2	0-1	1-3		2-0	1-2	0-1	0-0	1-6	2-1	2-3	1-0	2-0	1-2	1-0	0-0
Hitchin Town	3-1	1-0	1-1	1-0	1-1	1-3	4-3	2-1	0-1	2-0	2-2	3-0		0-0	5-0	2-0	0-1	4-2	2-3	4-1	4-1	1-0	1-0	1-1
Kettering Town	2-2	2-1	3-1	0-0	1-0	3-1	2-3	1-0	1-3	4-1	1-1	0-0	1-1		1-0	1-1	1-2	3-0	1-1	1-2	2-0	0-3	1-1	3-1
King's Lynn Town	1-0	2-1	1-2	1-1	3-1	4-0	3-0	1-1	3-3	0-1	1-1	2-2	1-2	1-2		1-1	0-0	1-1	2-1	5-2	2-1	1-2	2-0	1-6
Kings Langley	0-1	2-0	4-5	2-0	1-2	1-1	0-1	1-0	2-0	0-1	2-2	1-0	1-2	1-2	2-2		0-2	2-2	1-2	2-3	2-3	1-3	1-1	1-1
Leamington	1-0	3-1	1-1	1-0	2-0	1-1	6-0	3-1	5-0	5-0	1-0	2-1	3-0	3-0	0-0	3-0		1-0	6-0	2-0	2-0	1-1	2-0	1-1
Merthyr Town	1-0	4-0	1-0	5-0	1-0	2-2	2-0	3-0	2-0	4-3	1-2	4-0	2-2	2-0	1-1	5-0	1-1		2-0	1-1	2-0	3-0	1-1	2-2
Redditch United	0-0	2-2	0-2	1-2	3-1	0-2	2-2	4-1	4-2	1-0	2-1	2-1	1-2	1-3	1-1	0-0	0-0	0-2		0-4	0-2	1-4	1-1	2-1
Slough Town	2-0	3-2	3-0	1-0	1-2	0-1	4-1	0-2	2-1	1-0	1-2	3-2	0-1	3-2	2-2	2-0	1-0	1-1	3-0		2-0	0-0	3-0	3-0
St. Ives Town	1-1	0-1	0-1	0-0	0-2	2-3	1-1	1-1	0-1	1-0	3-1	4-1	0-3	0-7	2-0	2-1	0-5	0-0	1-1	2-0		2-1	1-1	1-2
St. Neots Town	1-4	2-1	0-5	0-3	4-1	3-3	3-1	1-1	3-2	2-0	3-2	1-5	1-2	1-5	5-2	5-2	0-1	2-3	1-0	1-1	0-4		1-1	0-4
Stratford Town	2-0	1-1	1-0	3-3	1-1	0-1	4-2	0-1	1-1	2-0	3-0	0-0	3-2	4-1	1-1	2-2	0-2	0-3	2-4	1-2	2-3	5-2		0-5
Weymouth	2-2	3-0	2-2	2-0	2-0	1-4	3-0	4-0	2-1	3-3	2-1	2-2	0-2	3-2	0-0	1-1	4-0	0-1	1-0	0-1	1-1	0-2	1-1	

Evo-Stik Southern Premier
Premier Division

Season 2016/2017

Team	P	W	D	L	F	A	Pts
Chippenham Town	46	31	10	5	94	47	103
Leamington	46	27	14	5	92	42	95
Merthyr Town	46	25	14	7	92	42	89
Hitchin Town	46	24	14	8	79	45	86
Slough Town	46	26	7	13	84	56	85
Banbury United	46	24	8	14	67	40	80
Biggleswade Town	46	21	11	14	85	59	74
Frome Town	46	20	14	12	80	67	74
Kettering Town	46	21	10	15	84	66	73
Weymouth	46	16	18	12	79	58	66
Chesham United	46	18	10	18	67	62	64
Basingstoke Town	46	18	8	20	65	72	62
King's Lynn Town	46	14	18	14	60	69	60
Stratford Town	46	13	17	16	64	66	56
St. Ives Town	46	15	11	20	49	70	56
Dunstable Town	46	16	6	24	46	65	54
Redditch United	46	13	11	22	54	75	50
Dorchester Town	46	12	12	22	52	80	48
St. Neots Town	46	14	6	26	66	101	48
Kings Langley	46	11	14	21	57	72	47
Cambridge City	46	12	11	23	46	72	47
Cirencester Town	46	11	9	26	54	92	42
Hayes & Yeading United	46	10	11	25	48	81	41
Cinderford Town	46	8	3	35	49	106	27

Promotion Play-offs

Leamington	1	Slough Town	0	
Merthyr Town	1	Hitchin Town	1	(aet)

Hitchin Town won 4-1 on penalties

Leamington	2	Hitchin Town	1	(aet)

Promoted: Chippenham Town and Leamington

Relegated: Cambridge City, Cirencester Town, Hayes & Yeading United and Cinderford Town

Isthmian League Premier Divison 2016/2017 Season

	AFC Sudbury	Billericay Town	Bognor Regis Town	Burgess Hill Town	Canvey Island	Dulwich Hamlet	Enfield Town	Folkestone Invicta	Grays Athletic	Harlow Town	Harrow Borough	Havant & Waterlooville	Hendon	Kingstonian	Leatherhead	Leiston	Lowestoft Town	Merstham	Metropolitan Police	Needham Market	Staines Town	Tonbridge Angels	Wingate & Finchley	Worthing
AFC Sudbury		2-3	0-4	3-0	1-1	2-2	2-0	3-1	5-1	1-2	1-3	0-2	0-4	1-1	1-2	1-3	1-1	0-4	3-0	1-1	3-1	0-1	2-2	1-0
Billericay Town	2-3		0-2	4-0	3-1	0-2	2-4	1-0	2-0	1-1	2-1	0-2	4-1	0-2	4-2	2-0	0-1	1-1	1-1	6-0	1-0	2-1	3-0	3-0
Bognor Regis Town	2-1	2-1		1-1	4-0	1-1	1-1	7-1	1-2	3-0	1-0	1-1	0-2	2-0	1-0	1-0	1-3	2-0	1-1	2-1	2-0	2-0	3-1	5-0
Burgess Hill Town	2-0	2-1	1-3		1-1	0-3	1-0	4-2	2-1	0-1	5-1	3-3	1-0	2-1	3-2	0-6	1-3	2-1	1-4	0-3	3-3	1-2	2-3	0-1
Canvey Island	2-2	1-2	0-5	2-1		1-0	1-5	1-3	3-1	1-1	3-0	1-2	3-1	1-2	3-0	2-3	3-0	2-2	1-2	2-2	0-6	0-1	1-4	2-0
Dulwich Hamlet	2-0	0-3	1-3	2-2	1-2		2-1	6-1	0-1	3-1	1-4	3-0	2-1	4-2	1-1	2-4	3-1	5-0	3-3	2-0	3-1	1-2	1-1	4-1
Enfield Town	1-0	2-2	1-0	0-1	1-1	2-2		3-1	2-0	3-0	0-1	1-4	6-0	3-0	2-1	1-1	2-2	2-3	1-0	3-3	2-1	3-1	0-1	2-1
Folkestone Invicta	4-2	1-0	1-2	3-1	6-0	1-1	2-0		0-1	1-4	3-0	1-3	1-2	3-1	1-1	2-0	4-1	0-0	2-0	0-1	1-1	1-0	1-0	2-4
Grays Athletic	1-3	1-0	1-1	1-1	2-0	0-2	1-3	0-3		3-1	2-5	0-2	1-2	2-1	1-2	1-1	0-3	1-0	0-2	1-2	2-2	0-2	1-2	1-4
Harlow Town	1-3	0-2	3-1	2-2	2-2	1-2	0-3	2-2	5-0		2-0	2-0	1-0	2-1	1-2	1-2	2-1	3-1	5-1	1-0			3-0	6-2
Harrow Borough	1-1	0-0	0-1	0-2	1-0	0-2	1-5	4-1	1-3	2-0		2-1	0-2	0-4	3-1	3-1	4-1	1-0						
Havant & Waterlooville	6-0	1-2	1-0	1-0	4-0	2-1	0-2	1-0	5-0	5-2	3-1		3-2	1-1	3-1	0-0	1-0	3-0	1-2	1-3	1-1	2-0	1-1	3-2
Hendon	1-2	1-0	2-2	1-1	0-0	1-1	1-1	3-3	0-4	2-2	4-5	1-1		1-4	1-3	2-1	0-0	2-1	2-0	2-1	1-1	1-2	0-1	0-3
Kingstonian	3-0	0-3	1-2	2-0	3-1	0-1	0-2	2-2	2-1	0-1	2-3	0-0	1-1		1-2	4-2	2-5	2-1	2-1	1-2	3-2	0-3	0-2	1-3
Leatherhead	2-0	3-2	1-3	1-2	1-1	2-2	2-1	2-0	1-1	3-2	2-2	2-3		3-2		3-3	3-1	3-0	2-1	1-1	1-0	0-0	1-0	1-1
Leiston	2-1	4-1	1-1	2-0	4-0	2-2	1-1	2-1	4-1	5-2	2-2	3-1	2-3	4-4	1-0		1-2	1-2	4-0	5-1	0-1	2-0	1-2	2-0
Lowestoft Town	2-2	1-1	2-1	1-0	0-3	0-3	2-1	2-2	2-1	4-0	2-0	0-2	3-3	1-0	1-0	3-2		1-5	0-1	1-1	1-3	0-1	2-1	0-4
Merstham	0-1	1-1	1-1	2-2	0-3	1-4	2-2	3-1	6-1	1-0	5-0	3-4	0-1	0-0	2-1	1-0	2-1		2-1	4-1	0-0	5-3	0-2	1-2
Metropolitan Police	1-0	1-1	0-1	2-1	0-4	1-1	3-0	1-0	3-1	0-2	1-1	1-2	1-2	1-0	0-1	2-1	2-2	0-2		2-1	1-6	1-1	2-0	1-3
Needham Market	2-1	1-2	2-2	1-1	3-3	1-1	1-3	2-1	5-1	2-1	2-1	0-0	5-2	2-1	2-1	0-4	2-1	1-1	1-0		1-1	0-2	1-0	2-1
Staines Town	4-0	3-2	0-2	1-2	1-1	2-0	2-2	0-2	3-0	0-2	1-4	3-2	0-2	2-5	2-3	2-1	3-0	3-2	4-1	1-1		0-0	0-1	4-0
Tonbridge Angels	1-0	1-0	4-1	0-0	3-0	0-0	3-0	2-2	4-1	0-3	1-0	1-1	3-1	0-1	4-4	2-2	1-0	2-2	2-1	3-4	1-2		3-0	2-1
Wingate & Finchley	4-1	1-2	0-2	2-1	1-2	0-3	1-5	3-2	1-0	0-0	3-1	0-2	1-0	2-1	2-1	1-0	1-1	3-2	2-3	0-1	1-1	4-0		1-0
Worthing	0-0	2-2	1-1	1-1	5-0	0-1	1-3	3-3	0-1	3-2	0-4	1-2	1-2	0-0	3-2	1-3	0-1	1-0	3-1	4-3	5-3	3-0	1-4	

Isthmian League Premier Division

Season 2016/2017

	P	W	D	L	F	A	Pts
Havant & Waterlooville	46	28	10	8	88	43	94
Bognor Regis Town	46	27	11	8	87	41	92
Dulwich Hamlet	46	22	14	10	89	55	80
Enfield Town	46	21	13	12	86	57	76
Wingate & Finchley	46	23	6	17	63	61	75
Tonbridge Angels	46	21	11	14	66	55	74
Leiston	46	21	10	15	98	66	73
Billericay Town	46	21	9	16	77	56	72
Needham Market	46	20	12	14	76	80	72
Harlow Town	46	20	7	19	76	72	67
Lowestoft Town	46	18	10	18	63	73	64
Staines Town	46	16	13	17	78	68	61
Leatherhead	46	16	12	18	72	72	57
Worthing	46	16	8	22	73	85	56
Folkestone Invicta	46	15	10	21	75	82	55
Kingstonian	46	16	7	23	65	73	55
Metropolitan Police	46	15	9	22	54	72	54
Hendon	46	14	12	20	68	88	54
Burgess Hill Town	46	14	12	20	59	80	54
Merstham	46	15	11	20	70	72	53
Harrow Borough	46	14	11	21	60	80	53
Canvey Island	46	13	13	20	63	92	52
AFC Sudbury	46	12	10	24	57	85	46
Grays Athletic	46	11	5	30	46	101	38

Leatherhead were deducted three points for fielding an ineligible player.
Merstham were deducted three points for fielding an ineligible player.
Harrow Borough were reprieved from relegation after Worcester City requested relegation to Level 5.

Promotion Play-offs

Bognor Regis Town 2   Wingate & Finchley 1
Dulwich Hamlet 4   Enfield Town 2

Bognor Regis Town 2   Dulwich Hamlet 1

Promoted: Havant & Waterlooville and Bognor Regis Town
Relegated: Canvey Island, AFC Sudbury and Grays Athletic

F.A. Trophy 2016/2017

Qualifying 1	AFC Rushden & Diamonds	1	Coalville Town	0
Qualifying 1	AFC Sudbury	4	Bowers & Pitsea	0
Qualifying 1	Ashton United	0	Marine	4
Qualifying 1	Bamber Bridge	0	Trafford	2
Qualifying 1	Banbury United	0	Bishop's Cleeve	1
Qualifying 1	Bedworth United	2	St Neots Town	3
Qualifying 1	Biggleswade Town	1	Witham Town	0
Qualifying 1	Billericay Town	2	Maldon & Tiptree	0
Qualifying 1	Burgess Hill Town	5	Beaconsfield SYCOB	1
Qualifying 1	Buxton	2	Glossop North End	0
Qualifying 1	Carlton Town	1	St Ives Town	4
Qualifying 1	Chalfont St Peter	3	Corinthian Casuals	2
Qualifying 1	Cheshunt	1	Folkestone Invicta	3
Qualifying 1	Cirencester Town	1	Havant & Waterlooville	2
Qualifying 1	Colwyn Bay	1	Witton Albion	1
Qualifying 1	Corby Town	0	Stafford Rangers	2
Qualifying 1	Cray Wanderers	4	Marlow	0
Qualifying 1	Dorchester Town	3	Barnstaple Town	1
Qualifying 1	East Grinstead Town	2	Phoenix Sports	3
Qualifying 1	Enfield Town	3	Canvey Island	2
Qualifying 1	Evesham United	1	Frome Town	1
Qualifying 1	Faversham Town	3	South Park	4
Qualifying 1	Fleet Town	1	Winchester City	2
Qualifying 1	Goole	1	Blyth Spartans	1
Qualifying 1	Grays Athletic	1	Wingate & Finchley	1
Qualifying 1	Hanwell Town	2	Bury Town	1
Qualifying 1	Hastings United	4	Aylesbury United	0
Qualifying 1	Hayes & Yeading United	0	Hitchin Town	1
Qualifying 1	Herne Bay	2	Harrow Borough	2
Qualifying 1	Horsham	1	Romford	3
Qualifying 1	Hythe Town	3	Walton Casuals	2
Qualifying 1	Ilkeston	0	Barwell	2
Qualifying 1	Kettering Town	5	Market Drayton Town	1
Qualifying 1	Kidsgrove Athletic	5	Soham Town Rangers	3
Qualifying 1	Kings Langley	1	Heybridge Swifts	0
Qualifying 1	Kingstonian	2	Lewes	1
Qualifying 1	Leamington	0	Mickleover Sports	1
Qualifying 1	Leatherhead	2	Chesham United	3
Qualifying 1	Leek Town	2	Sutton Coldfield Town	1
Qualifying 1	Leiston	5	Hendon	0
Qualifying 1	Lincoln United	4	Gresley	2
Qualifying 1	Lowestoft Town	1	Dulwich Hamlet	2
Qualifying 1	Merthyr Town	6	Cinderford Town	1
Qualifying 1	Metropolitan Police	2	Brightlingsea Regent	6
Qualifying 1	Mossley	1	Farsley Celtic	3
Qualifying 1	Needham Market	2	Wroxham	0
Qualifying 1	Ramsbottom United	2	Prescot Cables	1
Qualifying 1	Redditch United	3	Cambridge City	1
Qualifying 1	Royston Town	2	Northwood	2
Qualifying 1	Rushall Olympic	1	Halesowen Town	2
Qualifying 1	Salisbury	2	Chippenham Town	3
Qualifying 1	Shaw Lane Association	6	Frickley Athletic	2
Qualifying 1	Skelmersdale United	1	Kendal Town	3
Qualifying 1	Slough Town	4	Bognor Regis Town	1
Qualifying 1	Spennymoor Town	1	Matlock Town	2

Qualifying 1	Staines Town	1	Basingstoke Town	4
Qualifying 1	Stamford	1	Hednesford Town	4
Qualifying 1	Stocksbridge Park Steels	2	Lancaster City	1
Qualifying 1	Stourbridge	1	Kingýs Lynn Town	2
Qualifying 1	Stratford Town	2	Grantham Town	2
Qualifying 1	Taunton Town	5	Swindon Supermarine	0
Qualifying 1	Tiverton Town	0	Wimborne Town	1
Qualifying 1	Tonbridge Angels	3	Ashford Town (Middx)	3
Qualifying 1	Tooting & Mitcham United	2	Dunstable Town	4
Qualifying 1	Uxbridge	0	Harlow Town	1
Qualifying 1	VCD Athletic	1	Ware	3
Qualifying 1	Waltham Abbey	0	Merstham	5
Qualifying 1	Warrington Town	0	Nantwich Town	2
Qualifying 1	Weymouth	4	Wantage Town	0
Qualifying 1	Whitby Town	4	Workington	3
Qualifying 1	Worthing	3	Kempston Rovers	1
Qualifying 1	Yate Town	1	North Leigh	6
Replay	Ashford Town (Middx)	1	Tonbridge Angels	4
Replay	Blyth Spartans	7	Goole	1
Replay	Frome Town	1	Evesham United	0
Replay	Grantham Town	4	Stratford Town	0
Replay	Harrow Borough	3	Herne Bay	0
Replay	Northwood	1	Royston Town	4
Replay	Wingate & Finchley	2	Grays Athletic	0
Replay	Witton Albion	3	Colwyn Bay	1
Qualifying 2	AFC Rushden & Diamonds	3	Lincoln United	3
Qualifying 2	AFC Sudbury	4	Romford	0
Qualifying 2	Barwell	2	Farsley Celtic	3
Qualifying 2	Biggleswade Town	1	Hitchin Town	1
Qualifying 2	Bishopýs Cleeve	0	Taunton Town	1
Qualifying 2	Blyth Spartans	4	Halesowen Town	3
Qualifying 2	Brightlingsea Regent	1	Harlow Town	1
Qualifying 2	Burgess Hill Town	2	Chalfont St Peter	2
Qualifying 2	Buxton	1	Kingýs Lynn Town	3
Qualifying 2	Chippenham Town	0	Leiston	1
Qualifying 2	Cray Wanderers	1	Worthing	2
Qualifying 2	Dorchester Town	0	Basingstoke Town	3
Qualifying 2	Dulwich Hamlet	4	Chesham United	0
Qualifying 2	Dunstable Town	1	Weymouth	4
Qualifying 2	Folkestone Invicta	2	North Leigh	3
Qualifying 2	Grantham Town	0	Matlock Town	2
Qualifying 2	Hanwell Town	0	Frome Town	1
Qualifying 2	Hastings United	1	South Park	1
Qualifying 2	Havant & Waterlooville	5	Billericay Town	0
Qualifying 2	Hednesford Town	1	Stafford Rangers	1
Qualifying 2	Kidsgrove Athletic	3	Stocksbridge Park Steels	5
Qualifying 2	Kings Langley	1	Enfield Town	0
Qualifying 2	Kingstonian	1	Tonbridge Angels	1
Qualifying 2	Marine	1	St Neots Town	1
Qualifying 2	Merstham	0	Hythe Town	3
Qualifying 2	Merthyr Town	2	Slough Town	2
Qualifying 2	Nantwich Town	2	Kendal Town	0
Qualifying 2	Needham Market	1	Harrow Borough	2
Qualifying 2	Phoenix Sports	1	Winchester City	3
Qualifying 2	Ramsbottom United	4	Redditch United	1
Qualifying 2	Royston Town	4	Wimborne Town	0
Qualifying 2	Shaw Lane Association	3	Whitby Town	0

Qualifying 2	St Ives Town	2	Leek Town	1	
Qualifying 2	Trafford	0	Mickleover Sports	1	
Qualifying 2	Ware	0	Wingate & Finchley	2	
Qualifying 2	Witton Albion	2	Kettering Town	1	
Replay	Chalfont St Peter	1	Burgess Hill Town	1	(aet)
	Burgess Hill Town won 8-7 on penalties				
Replay	Harlow Town	2	Brightlingsea Regent	1	
Replay	Hitchin Town	3	Biggleswade Town	2	
Replay	Lincoln United	2	AFC Rushden & Diamonds	0	
Replay	Slough Town	2	Merthyr Town	0	
Replay	South Park	3	Hastings United	2	(aet)
Replay	St Neots Town	2	Marine	4	(aet)
Replay	Stafford Rangers	2	Hednesford Town	1	(aet)
Replay	Tonbridge Angels	1	Kingstonian	2	
Qualifying 3	Altrincham	2	Blyth Spartans	2	
Qualifying 3	Bath City	2	Basingstoke Town	0	
Qualifying 3	Burgess Hill Town	0	Hitchin Town	3	
Qualifying 3	Chelmsford City	1	Taunton Town	0	
Qualifying 3	Chorley	1	Stafford Rangers	0	
Qualifying 3	Concord Rangers	0	Welling United	1	
Qualifying 3	Curzon Ashton	1	Worcester City	2	
Qualifying 3	Darlington 1883	2	Marine	2	
Qualifying 3	Ebbsfleet United	4	Harrow Borough	2	
Qualifying 3	FC United Of Manchester	1	Nuneaton Town	5	
Qualifying 3	Farsley Celtic	2	Tamworth	2	
Qualifying 3	Gainsborough Trinity	0	Alfreton Town	0	
Qualifying 3	Gloucester City	2	AFC Fylde	3	
Qualifying 3	Hampton & Richmond Borough	0	Royston Town	0	
Qualifying 3	Harrogate Town	2	Salford City	2	
Qualifying 3	Havant & Waterlooville	1	Harlow Town	3	
Qualifying 3	Hungerford Town	0	Gosport Borough	1	
Qualifying 3	Hythe Town	4	Bishopýs Stortford	2	
Qualifying 3	Kidderminster Harriers	3	Lincoln United	1	
Qualifying 3	Kings Langley	1	AFC Sudbury	3	
Qualifying 3	Kingýs Lynn Town	1	St Ives Town	0	
Qualifying 3	Leiston	1	Eastbourne Borough	1	
Qualifying 3	Maidenhead United	2	Wealdstone	2	
Qualifying 3	Margate	1	East Thurrock United	1	
Qualifying 3	Matlock Town	1	FC Halifax Town	1	
Qualifying 3	Mickleover Sports	1	Brackley Town	1	
Qualifying 3	North Leigh	1	Kingstonian	0	
Qualifying 3	Oxford City	1	South Park	2	
Qualifying 3	Poole Town	1	Weymouth	1	
Qualifying 3	Ramsbottom United	0	AFC Telford United	2	
Qualifying 3	Shaw Lane Association	3	Nantwich Town	1	
	Shaw Lane Association was subsequently disqualified for fielding an ineligible player.				
Qualifying 3	Slough Town	2	Wingate & Finchley	4	
Qualifying 3	Stockport County	2	Bradford (Park Avenue)	0	
Qualifying 3	Stocksbridge Park Steels	2	Stalybridge Celtic	2	
Qualifying 3	Truro City	6	Frome Town	1	
Qualifying 3	Weston Super Mare	2	Dartford	4	
Qualifying 3	Whitehawk	1	St Albans City	1	
Qualifying 3	Winchester City	0	Dulwich Hamlet	1	
Qualifying 3	Witton Albion	4	Boston United	2	
Qualifying 3	Worthing	1	Hemel Hempstead Town	1	
Replay	Alfreton Town	4	Gainsborough Trinity	1	(aet)

Replay	Blyth Spartans	2	Altrincham	3	
Replay	Brackley Town	3	Mickleover Sports	1	
Replay	East Thurrock United	2	Margate	0	
Replay	Eastbourne Borough	2	Leiston	2	(aet)
	Leiston won 5-3 on penalties				
Replay	FC Halifax Town	2	Matlock Town	3	
Replay	Hemel Hempstead Town	0	Worthing	1	
Replay	Marine	3	Darlington 1883	2	
Replay	Royston Town	2	Hampton & Richmond Borough	1	
Replay	Salford City	0	Harrogate Town	3	
Replay	St Albans City	0	Whitehawk	1	
Replay	Stalybridge Celtic	2	Stocksbridge Park Steels	3	
Replay	Tamworth	0	Farsley Celtic	4	
Replay	Wealdstone	2	Maidenhead United	1	
Replay	Weymouth	2	Poole Town	0	
Round 1	AFC Fylde	1	Brackley Town	1	
Round 1	AFC Sudbury	2	Gosport Borough	1	
Round 1	Alfreton Town	1	North Ferriby United	0	
Round 1	Altrincham	1	Macclesfield Town	1	
Round 1	Boreham Wood	0	Maidstone United	0	
Round 1	Braintree Town	2	Torquay United	0	
Round 1	Bromley	1	Leiston	1	
Round 1	Chelmsford City	1	Hitchin Town	0	
Round 1	Chorley	0	Guiseley	1	
Round 1	Dagenham & Redbridge	1	Worthing	2	
Round 1	Dartford	1	Dover Athletic	1	
Round 1	Dulwich Hamlet	2	Royston Town	2	
Round 1	East Thurrock United	1	Aldershot Town	1	
Round 1	Ebbsfleet United	1	Woking	1	
Round 1	Farsley Celtic	0	Southport	4	
Round 1	Forest Green Rovers	1	Truro City	1	
Round 1	Gateshead	2	Kingś Lynn Town	0	
Round 1	Harlow Town	2	Eastleigh	0	
Round 1	Harrogate Town	3	Barrow	3	
Round 1	Kidderminster Harriers	4	AFC Telford United	0	
Round 1	Nantwich Town	1	Lincoln City	2	
Round 1	Nuneaton Town	3	Stocksbridge Park Steels	1	
Round 1	Solihull Moors	1	Matlock Town	2	
Round 1	South Park	1	North Leigh	1	
Round 1	Stockport County	3	Marine	2	
Round 1	Sutton United	1	Bath City	0	
Round 1	Wealdstone	2	Wingate & Finchley	2	
Round 1	Welling United	8	Hythe Town	1	
Round 1	Whitehawk	2	Weymouth	2	
Round 1	Witton Albion	1	Chester	1	
Round 1	Wrexham	0	Tranmere Rovers	1	
Round 1	York City	3	Worcester City	1	
Replay	Aldershot Town	3	East Thurrock United	4	(aet)
Replay	Barrow	4	Harrogate Town	2	(aet)
Replay	Brackley Town	4	AFC Fylde	0	
Replay	Chester	2	Witton Albion	1	
Replay	Dover Athletic	1	Dartford	2	
Replay	Leiston	3	Bromley	5	
Replay	Macclesfield Town	2	Altrincham	1	
Replay	Maidstone United	2	Boreham Wood	3	
Replay	North Leigh	1	South Park	3	

Replay	Royston Town	0	Dulwich Hamlet	1	
Replay	Truro City	0	Forest Green Rovers	1	(aet)
Replay	Weymouth	1	Whitehawk	2	
Replay	Wingate & Finchley	1	Wealdstone	2	(aet)
Replay	Woking	0	Ebbsfleet United	1	
Round 2	AFC Sudbury	1	Macclesfield Town	3	
Round 2	Barrow	3	Matlock Town	2	
Round 2	Boreham Wood	2	Alfreton Town	1	
Round 2	Bromley	1	Welling United	2	
Round 2	Chester	0	Forest Green Rovers	2	
Round 2	Dartford	0	Chelmsford City	1	
Round 2	East Thurrock United	2	Braintree Town	5	
Round 2	Gateshead	1	Lincoln City	3	
Round 2	Harlow Town	1	York City	2	
Round 2	Kidderminster Harriers	3	Ebbsfleet United	0	
Round 2	Nuneaton Town	6	Guiseley	1	
Round 2	Southport	1	Wealdstone	2	
Round 2	Stockport County	1	Brackley Town	1	
Round 2	Tranmere Rovers	4	South Park	1	
Round 2	Whitehawk	1	Dulwich Hamlet	4	
Round 2	Worthing	2	Sutton United	2	
Replay	Brackley Town	2	Stockport County	0	
Replay	Sutton United	3	Worthing	2	(aet)
Round 3	Barrow	1	Kidderminster Harriers	0	
Round 3	Braintree Town	0	Dulwich Hamlet	0	
Round 3	Macclesfield Town	1	Forest Green Rovers	0	
Round 3	Nuneaton Town	0	York City	3	
Round 3	Sutton United	0	Boreham Wood	0	
Round 3	Tranmere Rovers	1	Chelmsford City	1	
Round 3	Wealdstone	1	Brackley Town	4	
Round 3	Welling United	1	Lincoln City	3	
Replay	Boreham Wood	5	Sutton United	0	
Replay	Chelmsford City	1	Tranmere Rovers	4	
Replay	Dulwich Hamlet	5	Braintree Town	2	
Round 4	Boreham Wood	0	Lincoln City	2	
Round 4	Dulwich Hamlet	2	Macclesfield Town	2	
Round 4	Tranmere Rovers	5	Barrow	1	
Round 4	York City	1	Brackley Town	0	
Replay	Macclesfield Town	2	Dulwich Hamlet	0	
Semi-finals					
1st leg	Macclesfield Town	1	Tranmere Rovers	1	
2nd leg	Tranmere Rovers	0	Macclesfield Town	1	
	Macclesfield Town won 2-1 on aggregate				
1st leg	York City	2	Lincoln City	1	
2nd leg	Lincoln City	1	York City	1	(aet)
	York City won 3-2 on aggregate				
FINAL	York City	3	Macclesfield Town	2	

F.A. Vase 2016/2017

Round 1	1874 Northwich	1	Billingham Synthonia	0	
Round 1	AC London	3	Highworth Town	3	(aet)
Round 1	AFC Emley	3	Chadderton	1	
Round 1	AFC Liverpool	0	Bootle	6	
Round 1	AFC Stoneham	1	Shaftesbury Town	3	
Round 1	Abbey Rangers	3	Tunbridge Wells	0	
Round 1	Abingdon United	1	Thatcham Town	3	
Round 1	Alresford Town	5	Lingfield	3	
Round 1	Alton Town	0	Corinthian	2	
Round 1	Amesbury Town	0	Brimscombe & Thrupp	1	
Round 1	Ash United	0	Chichester City	4	
Round 1	Ashby Ivanhoe	3	Hucknall Town	4	(aet)
Round 1	Ashton Town	0	Billingham Town	4	
Round 1	Atherton Collieries	5	Jarrow Roofing Boldon CA	0	
Round 1	Atherton LR	0	Chester-Le-Street Town	3	
Round 1	Banstead Athletic	1	Crowborough Athletic	3	
Round 1	Beckenham Town	1	Lancing	3	
Round 1	Bedfont Sports	5	Buckingham Town	4	
Round 1	Bemerton Heath Harlequins	2	Plymouth Parkway	2	(aet)
Round 1	Biggleswade United	2	Baldock Town	1	
Round 1	Bottesford Town	2	Haughmond	0	
Round 1	Bournemouth	0	Melksham Town	3	
Round 1	Bridlington Town	0	Pickering Town	1	
Round 1	Broadfields United	2	London Bari	1	
Round 1	Bromsgrove Sporting	5	Cadbury Athletic	3	(aet)
Round 1	Calne Town	0	Torpoint Athletic	2	
Round 1	Canning Town	4	Biggleswade	5	(aet)
Round 1	Canterbury City	3	Lydney Town	1	
Round 1	Charnock Richard	3	Barnoldswick Town	1	(aet)
Round 1	Clevedon Town	4	Willand Rovers	2	(aet)
Round 1	Colney Heath	1	Hoddesdon Town	4	
Round 1	Congleton Town	2	Hall Road Rangers	3	
Round 1	Coventry Copsewood	0	Holbeach United	2	
Round 1	Crawley Green	1	Basildon United	2	
Round 1	Cribbs	1	Odd Down	1	
Round 1	Croydon	4	Bracknell Town	1	
Round 1	Cullompton Rangers	1	Hengrove Athletic	0	
Round 1	Daventry Town	2	Newport Pagnell Town	3	
Round 1	Devizes Town	0	Gillingham Town	3	
Round 1	Eastbourne Town	9	Tooting & Mitcham Wanderers	0	
Round 1	Eastbourne United	2	Horley Town	0	
Round 1	Epsom & Ewell	1	Bridon Ropes	0	
Round 1	Exmouth	3	Tavistock	2	
Round 1	FC Elmstead	0	Sporting Club Thamesmead	2	
Round 1	Fairford Town	1	Andover Town	2	
Round 1	Felixstowe & Walton United	4	Haverhill Borough	0	
Round 1	Flackwell Heath	0	Cockfosters	3	
Round 1	Godmanchester Rovers	0	London Colney	3	
Round 1	Gorleston	2	Barking	0	
Round 1	Guisborough Town	0	Padiham	3	
Round 1	Handsworth Parramore	3	Shepshed Dynamo	4	
Round 1	Heanor Town	0	Blidworth Welfare	4	
Round 1	Helston Athletic	1	Team Solent	2	
Round 1	Highmoor Ibis	0	Holmer Green	1	
Round 1	Hinckley	3	Wolverhampton SC	1	(aet)

Round 1	Holker Old Boys	1	Stockton Town	2	
Round 1	Hollands & Blair	0	Ascot United	1	
Round 1	Holwell Sports	0	AFC Mansfield	2	
Round 1	Horsham YMCA	3	Horndean	2	
Round 1	Kirby Muxloe	0	Hemsworth MW	1	
Round 1	Lichfield City	2	Shawbury United	1	
Round 1	Litherland Remyca	1	Shildon	4	
Round 1	Long Eaton United	2	Coventry United	1	
Round 1	Lordswood	1	Newhaven	2	
Round 1	Malvern Town	1	Worksop Town	2	
Round 1	Newcastle Benfield	3	Irlam	1	
Round 1	Northampton On Chenecks	1	Ely City	3	
Round 1	Northampton Sileby Rangers	5	Oxhey Jets	0	
Round 1	Penistone Church	1	Sherwood Colliery	2	
Round 1	Penrith	3	Easington Colliery	1	
Round 1	Peterborough Northern Star	1	Sun Sports	3	
Round 1	Peterborough Sports	6	Swaffham Town	0	
Round 1	Radford	3	Harborough Town	1	(aet)
Round 1	Rocester	8	Oakham United	1	
Round 1	Romsey Town	2	Portland United	3	
Round 1	Runcorn Town	1	Hallam	2	
Round 1	Shifnal Town	1	Quorn	4	
Round 1	Sholing	0	Buckland Athletic	3	
Round 1	Shoreham	2	Glebe	3	
Round 1	South Shields	2	Runcorn Linnets	1	
Round 1	Sporting Bengal United	0	Southall	3	
Round 1	Sporting Khalsa	1	Hanley Town	0	
Round 1	St Andrews	1	Paget Rangers	2	
Round 1	St Margaretsbury	3	Ilford	2	
Round 1	Staveley MW	2	Pinxton	0	
Round 1	Stockton Town	1	Sunderland Ryhope CW	3	
Round 1	Street	0	Blackfield & Langley	2	
Round 1	Thetford Town	2	Great Yarmouth Town	1	
Round 1	Thrapston Town	3	Leverstock Green	7	
Round 1	Tuffley Rovers	4	Sherborne Town	0	
Round 1	Uttoxeter Town	5	Leicester Road	4	
Round 1	Wadham Lodge	2	Hertford Town	1	
Round 1	Walsham Le Willows	0	Tring Athletic	1	
Round 1	Waltham Forest	1	Rothwell Corinthians	2	
Round 1	Walton & Hersham	3	Thame United	0	
Round 1	Welwyn Garden City	3	Saffron Walden Town	1	
Round 1	Wembley	5	Desborough Town	2	
Round 1	Westfields	6	Walsall Wood	0	
Round 1	Wick	0	Haywards Heath Town	1	
Round 1	Wolverhampton Casuals	2	Chelmsley Town	1	
Round 1	Yaxley	0	Stanway Rovers	1	
Replay	Highworth Town	2	AC London	1	
Replay	Odd Down	2	Cribbs	1	
Replay	Plymouth Parkway	0	Bemerton Heath Harlequins	3	
Round 2	1874 Northwich	0	Atherton Collieries	3	
Round 2	AFC Emley	1	Cleethorpes Town	2	
Round 2	Alvechurch	1	Sporting Khalsa	2	
Round 2	Basildon United	3	Felixstowe & Walton United	2	
Round 2	Bedfont Sports	2	Haywards Heath Town	0	

Round 2	Berkhamsted	5	Hullbridge Sports	2	
Round 2	Biggleswade United	1	Sun Sports	1	(aet)
Round 2	Billingham Town	5	Sunderland Ryhope CW	2	
Round 2	Blidworth Welfare	1	AFC Mansfield	2	
Round 2	Brimscombe & Thrupp	2	Bradford Town	2	(aet)
Round 2	Bristol Manor Farm	2	Odd Down	1	
Round 2	Bromsgrove Sporting	3	Lichfield City	1	
Round 2	Buckland Athletic	1	Newport (IOW)	0	
Round 2	Camberley Town	0	Southall	4	
Round 2	Charnock Richard	2	Staveley MW	4	(aet)
Round 2	Chichester City	3	Canterbury City	1	(aet)
Round 2	Cockfosters	1	Wembley	2	
Round 2	Corinthian	3	Alresford Town	2	
Round 2	Croydon	2	Andover Town	1	
Round 2	Cullompton Rangers	1	Bemerton Heath Harlequins	1	(aet)
Round 2	Dunston UTS	3	Hemsworth MW	1	
Round 2	Eastbourne Town	2	Ashford United	1	
Round 2	Eastbourne United	0	Crowborough Athletic	1	
Round 2	Epsom & Ewell	2	Abbey Rangers	3	
Round 2	FC Romania	2	Ipswich Wanderers	0	
Round 2	Gillingham Town	0	Exmouth	1	
Round 2	Gorleston	2	Northampton Sileby Rangers	1	
Round 2	Hall Road Rangers	0	Bottesford Town	2	
Round 2	Hallam	0	Morpeth Town	4	
Round 2	Hartley Wintney	1	Melksham Town	2	
Round 2	Highworth Town	1	Knaphill	3	
Round 2	Hoddesdon Town	2	Thetford Town	0	
Round 2	Hucknall Town	5	Rocester	1	
Round 2	Lancing	1	Horsham YMCA	7	
Round 2	Leverstock Green	1	Welwyn Garden City	2	
Round 2	London Colney	3	Holmer Green	0	
Round 2	Long Eaton United	3	Holbeach United	2	
Round 2	Moneyfields	0	Thatcham Town	4	
Round 2	Newcastle Benfield	0	Penrith	1	
Round 2	Newhaven	2	Ascot United	1	
Round 2	Newport Pagnell Town	2	Broadfields United	1	
Round 2	Newton Aycliffe	4	Worksop Town	0	
Round 2	North Shields	2	Chester-Le-Street Town	0	
Round 2	Padiham	0	Bootle	2	
Round 2	Paget Rangers	1	Hinckley	4	
Round 2	Peterborough Sports	5	Biggleswade	3	
Round 2	Pickering Town	0	Shildon	5	
Round 2	Portland United	1	Blackfield & Langley	2	
Round 2	Quorn	3	AFC Wulfrunians	1	(aet)
Round 2	Radford	1	Shepshed Dynamo	3	
Round 2	Rothwell Corinthians	1	Tring Athletic	2	
Round 2	Shaftesbury Town	1	Team Solent	3	
Round 2	Sleaford Town	4	Leicester Nirvana	1	
Round 2	South Shields	2	Marske United	0	
Round 2	St Margaretsbury	4	Stanway Rovers	2	(aet)
Round 2	Sunderland RCA	1	Stockton Town	0	(aet)
Round 2	Sutton Common Rovers	2	Sporting Club Thamesmead	1	
Round 2	Torpoint Athletic	1	Clevedon Town	0	
Round 2	Tuffley Rovers	0	Bodmin Town	2	
Round 2	Uttoxeter Town	1	Coleshill Town	3	

Round 2	Wadham Lodge	0	Ely City	3	
Round 2	Walton & Hersham	2	Glebe	2	(aet)
	Glebe won 3-1 on penalties				
Round 2	Westfields	3	Sherwood Colliery	2	
Round 2	Wolverhampton Casuals	1	Nuneaton Griff	2	
Replay	Bemerton Heath Harlequins	3	Cullompton Rangers	2	
Replay	Bradford Town	5	Brimscombe & Thrupp	0	
Replay	Sun Sports	1	Biggleswade United	1	(aet)
	Sun Sports won 5-4 on penalties				
Round 3	Abbey Rangers	1	Eastbourne Town	2	
Round 3	Bemerton Heath Harlequins	2	Melksham Town	3	
Round 3	Bottesford Town	1	Billingham Town	2	
Round 3	Bradford Town	2	Torpoint Athletic	0	
Round 3	Bristol Manor Farm	4	Thatcham Town	1	
Round 3	Cleethorpes Town	2	Bootle	1	
Round 3	Coleshill Town	4	Westfields	1	
Round 3	Crowborough Athletic	2	Bedfont Sports	2	(aet)
Round 3	Croydon	3	Glebe	2	
Round 3	Dunston UTS	1	Sunderland RCA	3	
Round 3	Exmouth	5	Blackfield & Langley	0	
Round 3	FC Romania	1	Tring Athletic	1	(aet)
Round 3	Gorleston		Basildon United		

The match was abandoned with four minutes to play after a spectator fell ill and, despite treatment from an attending air ambulance, subsequently died. Basildon United decided to forfeit the tie rather than appear in a replay.

Round 3	Hinckley	2	Quorn	1	(aet)
Round 3	Horsham YMCA	0	Buckland Athletic	3	
Round 3	Hucknall Town	1	AFC Mansfield	2	
Round 3	Knaphill	1	Southall	2	
Round 3	Long Eaton United	2	Shepshed Dynamo	4	(aet)
Round 3	Newhaven	1	Chichester City	3	
Round 3	Newport Pagnell Town	3	London Colney	1	
Round 3	Newton Aycliffe	2	Morpeth Town	3	
Round 3	North Shields	1	Shildon	2	
Round 3	Nuneaton Griff	0	Bromsgrove Sporting	2	
Round 3	Penrith	0	Atherton Collieries	3	
Round 3	South Shields	3	Staveley MW	0	
Round 3	Sporting Khalsa	5	Sleaford Town	5	(aet)
Round 3	St Margaretsbury	1	Berkhamsted	3	
Round 3	Sun Sports	3	Hoddesdon Town	1	
Round 3	Sutton Common Rovers	1	Corinthian	4	
Round 3	Team Solent	1	Bodmin Town	0	
Round 3	Welwyn Garden City	2	Ely City	3	
Round 3	Wembley	0	Peterborough Sports	4	
Replay	Bedfont Sports	2	Crowborough Athletic	3	
Replay	Sleaford Town	0	Sporting Khalsa	3	
Replay	Tring Athletic	2	FC Romania	1	
Round 4	AFC Mansfield	0	Sunderland RCA	1	
Round 4	Billingham Town	1	Cleethorpes Town	2	
Round 4	Bradford Town	2	Southall	4	(aet)
Round 4	Bristol Manor Farm	1	Melksham Town	1	(aet)
Round 4	Chichester City	1	Buckland Athletic	3	
Round 4	Crowborough Athletic	6	Eastbourne Town	0	
Round 4	Ely City	3	Shepshed Dynamo	0	
Round 4	Exmouth	4	Corinthian	0	

Round 4	Gorleston	0	Coleshill Town	3	
Round 4	Hinckley	5	Berkhamsted	0	
Round 4	Morpeth Town	0	South Shields	4	
Round 4	Newport Pagnell Town	3	Peterborough Sports	2	
Round 4	Shildon	1	Atherton Collieries	4	
Round 4	Sporting Khalsa	1	Tring Athletic	0	
Round 4	Sun Sports	0	Bromsgrove Sporting	4	
Round 4	Team Solent	3	Croydon	0	
Replay	Melksham Town	3	Bristol Manor Farm	5	
Round 5	Bromsgrove Sporting	2	Bristol Manor Farm	1	
Round 5	Cleethorpes Town	3	Atherton Collieries	2	
Round 5	Crowborough Athletic	3	Coleshill Town	6	
Round 5	Ely City	0	Sporting Khalsa	3	
Round 5	Hinckley	3	Buckland Athletic	4	(aet)
Round 5	Newport Pagnell Town	3	Sunderland RCA	2	(aet)
Round 5	Southall	4	Exmouth	2	
Round 5	Team Solent	2	South Shields	5	
Round 6	Bromsgrove Sporting	2	Buckland Athletic	0	
Round 6	Coleshill Town	2	Sporting Khalsa	0	
Round 6	South Shields	6	Newport Pagnell Town	1	
Round 6	Southall	2	Cleethorpes Town	5	

Semi-finals

1st leg	Bromsgrove Sporting	1	Cleethorpes Town	1	
2nd leg	Cleethorpes Town	1	Bromsgrove Sporting	0	
	Cleethorpes Town won 2-1 on aggregate				
1st leg	Coleshill Town	1	South Shields	2	
2nd leg	South Shields	4	Coleshill Town	0	
	South Shields won 6-1 on aggregate				
FINAL	South Shields	4	Cleethorpes Town	0	

	AFC Fylde	Aldershot Town	Barrow	Boreham Wood	Bromley	Chester	Dagenham & Redbridge	Dover Athletic	Eastleigh	Ebbsfleet United	FC Halifax Town	Gateshead	Guiseley	Hartlepool United	Leyton Orient	Macclesfield Town	Maidenhead United	Maidstone United	Solihull Moors	Sutton United	Torquay United	Tranmere Rovers	Woking	Wrexham
AFC Fylde		10/03	28/08	05/08	09/09	02/12	19/08	24/02	03/02	23/12	30/03	03/10	21/11	17/03	17/02	20/01	15/08	21/10	21/04	07/04	18/11	01/01	23/09	24/10
Aldershot Town	11/11		21/04	24/03	20/02	26/08	03/10	09/09	02/04	20/01	09/12	03/02	12/08	03/03	23/09	17/02	07/04	30/12	02/09	24/10	08/08	21/10	26/12	25/11
Barrow	02/04	28/10		02/09	25/11	28/04	09/12	24/03	03/03	14/04	08/08	20/02	12/09	10/02	07/10	11/11	26/08	30/09	30/12	27/01	16/09	06/01	12/08	26/12
Boreham Wood	09/12	19/08	30/03		28/10	14/04	08/08	20/01	03/10	23/09	07/10	17/02	28/04	11/11	09/09	03/03	03/02	20/02	12/08	26/12	30/12	17/03	25/11	28/08
Bromley	06/01	21/11	24/02	21/04		18/11	17/03	02/12	05/08	01/01	27/01	07/04	10/03	19/08	15/08	23/12	24/10	10/02	16/09	28/08	12/09	30/09	21/10	30/03
Chester	08/08	17/03	24/10	21/10	03/03		25/11	03/02	17/02	09/09	12/08	20/01	26/12	30/12	20/02	28/08	23/09	21/04	09/12	19/08	30/03	07/04	03/10	11/11
Dagenham & Red.	24/03	10/02	05/08	02/12	26/08	24/02		21/11	23/12	15/08	16/09	02/09	18/11	06/01	01/01	24/10	21/04	02/04	27/01	12/09	30/09	10/03	07/04	21/10
Dover Athletic	25/11	06/01	19/08	12/09	08/08	16/09	20/02		11/11	28/08	30/12	21/04	27/01	09/12	03/03	17/03	21/10	26/12	30/09	10/02	07/04	30/03	24/10	12/08
Eastleigh	16/09	28/08	18/11	10/02	09/12	30/09	12/08	10/03		30/03	24/02	21/10	06/01	27/01	17/03	21/04	21/11	12/09	24/10	08/08	26/12	19/08	30/12	07/04
Ebbsfleet United	12/08	12/09	21/10	27/01	26/12	06/01	30/12	02/04	02/09		30/09	26/08	09/12	25/11	11/11	07/04	24/03	08/08	10/02	21/04	24/10	16/09	20/02	03/03
FC Halifax Town	02/09	05/08	02/12	07/04	23/09	23/12	03/02	15/08	25/11	17/02		02/04	26/08	20/02	20/01	01/01	09/09	24/10	24/03	03/03	21/10	21/04	11/11	03/10
Gateshead	10/02	16/09	21/11	30/09	07/10	12/09	30/03	28/10	14/04	17/03	28/08		08/08	26/12	28/04	19/08	10/03	27/01	24/02	06/01	12/08	18/11	09/12	30/12
Guiseley	20/02	23/12	20/01	24/10	11/11	01/01	03/03	23/09	09/09	05/08	17/03	02/12		28/08	30/03	03/10	17/02	07/04	21/10	25/11	19/08	15/08	21/04	03/02
Hartlepool United	26/08	18/11	03/10	10/03	24/03	15/08	09/09	05/08	23/09	24/02	21/11	01/01	02/04		03/02	02/12	23/12	02/09	07/04	21/10	21/04	24/10	17/02	20/01
Leyton Orient	30/09	27/01	07/04	06/01	30/12	21/11	26/12	18/11	26/08	10/03	12/09	24/10	02/09	16/09		21/10	02/04	12/08	08/08	09/12	24/02	10/02	24/03	21/04
Macclesfield Town	12/09	30/09	10/03	18/11	12/08	02/04	28/04	26/08	28/10	07/10	26/12	24/03	10/02	08/08	14/04		24/02	16/09	06/01	30/12	27/01	21/11	02/09	09/12
Maidenhead United	30/12	07/10	17/03	16/09	28/04	27/01	28/10	14/04	20/02	19/08	06/01	11/11	30/09	12/08	28/08	25/11		09/12	26/12	30/03	10/02	12/09	03/03	08/08
Maidstone United	14/04	15/08	17/02	21/11	03/10	28/10	28/08	01/01	20/01	02/12	28/04	23/09	07/10	30/03	23/12	03/02	05/08		18/11	17/03	10/03	24/02	09/09	19/08
Solihull Moors	28/10	30/03	15/08	23/12	03/02	05/08	23/09	17/02	28/04	03/10	19/08	25/11	14/04	07/10	02/12	09/09	01/01	03/03		11/11	17/03	28/08	20/01	20/02
Sutton United	07/10	28/04	23/09	01/01	02/04	24/03	20/01	03/10	02/12	28/10	18/11	09/09	24/02	14/04	05/08	15/08	02/09	26/08	10/03		21/11	23/12	03/02	17/02
Torquay United	03/03	02/12	03/02	15/08	20/01	02/09	17/02	07/10	01/01	28/04	14/04	23/12	24/03	28/10	25/11	23/09	03/10	11/11	26/08	20/02		05/08	02/04	09/09
Tranmere Rovers	26/12	14/04	09/09	26/08	17/02	07/10	11/11	02/09	24/03	03/02	28/10	03/03	30/12	28/04	03/10	20/02	20/01	25/11	02/04	12/08	09/12		08/08	23/09
Woking	27/01	01/01	23/12	24/02	14/04	10/02	07/10	28/04	15/08	21/11	10/03	05/08	28/10	30/09	19/08	30/03	18/11	06/01	12/09	16/09	28/08	02/12		17/03
Wrexham	28/04	24/02	01/01	02/04	02/09	10/03	14/04	23/12	07/10	18/11	10/02	15/08	16/09	12/09	28/10	05/08	02/12	24/03	21/11	30/09	06/01	27/01	26/08	

Please note that the above fixtures may be subject to change.

National League North Fixtures 2017/2018	AFC Telford United	Alfreton Town	Blyth Spartans	Boston United	Brackley	Bradford Park Avenue	Chorley	Curzon Ashton	Darlington	FC United of Manchester	Gainsborough Trinity	Harrogate Town	Kidderminster Harriers	Leamington	North Ferriby United	Nuneaton Town	Salford City	Southport	Spennymoor Town	Stockport County	Tamworth	York City
AFC Telford United		18/11	02/09	07/10	08/08	26/08	07/04	06/01	24/03	24/02	21/04	09/09	26/12	02/04	10/02	20/01	12/08	28/10	10/03	12/09	04/11	09/12
Alfreton Town	03/03		05/08	23/12	12/09	02/12	07/10	28/08	13/01	21/04	09/09	28/10	17/03	20/01	15/08	31/03	17/02	19/08	07/04	01/01	10/02	11/11
Blyth Spartans	31/03	09/12		09/09	10/02	17/02	12/09	17/03	28/10	20/01	06/01	28/08	07/04	11/11	19/08	07/10	02/12	03/03	26/12	21/04	12/08	08/08
Boston United	28/04	08/08	27/01		28/10	14/04	19/08	10/02	23/09	17/03	26/12	03/03	31/03	17/02	05/09	28/08	14/10	09/12	12/08	11/11	06/01	02/12
Brackley	23/12	14/04	21/10	03/02		03/03	17/03	23/09	17/02	05/08	11/11	31/03	28/08	01/01	13/01	15/08	27/01	14/10	19/08	02/12	05/09	28/04
Bradford Park Avenue	17/03	10/03	04/11	11/09	18/11		28/08	26/12	10/02	19/08	20/01	21/04	07/10	07/04	24/02	09/09	28/10	07/08	06/01	31/03	09/12	12/08
Chorley	23/09	28/04	14/04	24/03	26/08	02/04		12/08	05/09	21/10	17/02	06/01	09/12	02/12	27/01	11/11	08/08	26/12	03/02	03/03	14/10	02/09
Curzon Ashton	14/08	02/04	26/08	21/10	07/04	01/01	13/01		02/12	09/09	03/02	07/10	20/01	11/09	05/08	03/03	02/09	11/11	21/04	23/12	24/03	17/02
Darlington	19/08	12/08	03/02	07/04	04/11	21/10	20/01	10/03		13/09	09/08	26/12	24/02	09/09	17/03	21/04	09/12	31/03	28/08	07/10	18/11	06/01
FC Utd of Manchester	11/11	14/10	05/09	26/08	09/12	24/03	10/02	27/01	14/04		03/03	02/12	12/08	02/09	28/04	28/10	26/12	06/01	08/08	17/02	23/09	02/04
Gainsborough Trinity	14/10	27/01	15/08	01/01	24/02	05/09	04/11	28/10	23/12	18/11		19/08	10/03	05/08	28/08	13/01	23/09	10/02	31/03	17/03	28/04	14/04
Harrogate Town	27/01	03/02	02/04	18/11	02/09	14/10	15/08	28/04	01/01	10/03	24/03		04/11	21/10	23/12	05/08	05/09	14/04	24/02	13/01	26/08	23/09
Kidderminster Harr.	01/01	26/08	23/09	02/09	02/04	28/04	05/08	05/09	11/11	13/01	02/12	17/02		15/08	14/10	23/12	24/03	27/01	21/10	03/02	14/04	03/03
Leamington	28/08	05/09	24/02	04/11	26/12	23/09	10/03	14/04	27/01	31/03	09/12	10/02	06/01		28/10	17/03	28/04	12/08	18/11	19/08	08/08	14/10
North Ferriby United	21/10	06/01	24/03	20/01	12/08	11/11	09/09	09/12	26/08	07/10	02/04	08/08	21/04	03/02		02/12	03/03	17/02	12/09	07/04	02/09	26/12
Nuneaton Town	05/09	02/09	28/04	02/04	06/01	27/01	24/02	18/11	14/10	03/02	12/08	09/12	08/08	26/08	10/03		14/04	23/09	04/11	21/10	26/12	24/03
Salford City	13/01	04/11	10/03	21/04	09/09	03/02	23/12	31/03	05/08	01/01	07/04	20/01	19/08	07/10	18/11	12/09		28/08	17/03	15/08	24/02	21/10
Southport	03/02	24/03	18/11	05/08	21/04	23/12	01/01	24/02	02/09	15/08	21/10	12/09	09/09	13/01	04/11	07/04	02/04		07/10	20/01	10/03	26/08
Spennymoor Town	02/12	23/09	01/01	13/01	24/03	15/08	28/10	14/10	02/04	23/12	02/09	11/11	10/02	03/03	14/04	17/02	26/08	28/04		05/08	27/01	05/09
Stockport County	14/04	26/12	14/10	24/02	10/03	02/09	18/11	08/08	28/04	04/11	26/08	12/08	28/10	24/03	23/09	10/02	06/01	05/09	09/12		02/04	27/01
Tamworth	17/02	21/10	13/01	15/08	20/01	05/08	21/04	19/08	03/03	07/04	07/10	17/03	12/09	23/12	31/03	01/01	11/11	02/12	09/09	28/08		03/02
York City	05/08	24/02	23/12	10/03	07/10	13/01	31/03	04/11	15/08	28/08	12/09	07/04	18/11	21/04	01/01	19/08	10/02	17/03	20/01	09/09	28/10	

Please note that the above fixtures may be subject to change.

National League South Fixtures 2017/2018	Bath City	Bognor Regis Town	Braintree Town	Chelmsford United	Chippenham Town	Concord Rangers	Dartford	Eastbourne Borough	East Thurrock United	Gloucester City	Hampton & Richmond Borough	Havant & Waterlooville	Hemel Hempstead	Hungerford Town	Oxford City	Poole Town	St. Albans City	Truro City	Wealdstone	Welling United	Weston-super-Mare	Whitehawk
Bath City		09/12	21/10	12/08	08/08	20/01	14/10	11/11	03/03	02/04	03/02	24/03	02/12	14/04	05/09	26/08	28/04	06/01	23/09	02/09	26/12	17/02
Bognor Regis Town	05/08		17/02	31/03	21/10	02/12	28/04	17/03	28/08	23/09	11/11	01/01	14/04	05/09	14/10	23/12	03/03	03/02	20/01	13/01	19/08	15/08
Braintree Town	10/02	04/11		26/12	12/08	14/04	08/08	06/01	09/12	28/04	19/08	28/10	20/01	23/09	31/03	24/02	28/08	14/10	10/03	05/09	18/11	17/03
Chelmsford City	13/01	02/09	01/01		03/02	02/04	21/10	11/09	07/10	05/08	27/01	21/04	17/02	02/12	11/11	07/04	14/08	26/08	24/03	23/12	09/09	03/03
Chippenham Town	23/12	10/02	13/01	28/10		03/03	20/01	19/08	31/03	05/09	17/02	05/08	23/09	01/01	28/08	15/08	11/11	14/04	14/10	28/04	17/03	02/12
Concord Rangers	09/09	10/03	12/09	28/08	18/11		06/01	26/12	27/01	04/11	07/04	07/10	08/08	31/03	03/02	21/04	17/03	12/08	09/12	24/02	21/10	19/08
Darlington	21/04	07/10	23/12	10/02	09/09	15/08		28/08	12/09	18/11	31/03	13/01	17/03	05/08	19/08	10/03	28/10	24/02	04/11	01/01	07/04	27/01
Eastbourne Borough	24/02	26/08	15/08	14/04	24/03	01/01	02/04		10/02	14/10	05/08	18/11	28/10	28/04	20/01	13/01	05/09	23/09	02/09	10/03	04/11	23/12
East Thurrock United	18/11	02/04	05/08	28/04	02/09	05/09	14/04	21/10		10/03	13/01	23/12	14/10	03/02	23/09	04/11	20/01	24/03	26/08	15/08	24/02	01/01
Gloucester City	28/08	07/04	07/10	09/12	27/01	17/02	03/03	21/04	02/12		11/09	09/09	19/08	17/03	26/12	03/02	31/03	07/08	12/08	21/10	06/01	11/11
Hampton & Richmond	28/10	24/02	24/03	05/09	04/11	23/09	02/09	09/12	12/08	14/04		26/08	06/01	20/01	08/08	18/11	14/10	28/04	26/12	02/04	10/03	10/02
Havant & Waterloo.	19/08	26/12	03/02	14/10	09/12	28/04	12/08	03/03	08/08	20/01	17/03		11/11	17/02	02/12	21/10	14/04	05/09	06/01	23/09	31/03	28/08
Hemel Hempstead T.	10/03	12/09	09/09	04/11	07/04	23/12	26/08	03/02	21/04	24/03	15/08	24/02		13/01	21/10	27/01	01/01	02/09	02/04	18/11	07/10	05/08
Hungerford Town	11/09	27/01	07/04	10/03	26/12	02/09	09/12	07/10	28/10	26/08	09/09	04/11	12/08		06/01	02/04	10/02	18/11	24/02	24/03	07/08	21/04
Oxford City	27/01	21/04	02/09	24/02	02/04	28/10	24/03	09/09	07/04	01/01	23/12	10/03	10/02	15/08		07/10	05/08	04/11	18/11	26/08	12/09	13/01
Poole Town	17/03	08/08	11/11	23/09	06/01	14/10	02/12	12/08	17/02	28/10	03/03	10/02	05/09	28/08	28/04		19/08	26/12	14/04	20/01	09/12	31/03
St. Albans City	07/10	18/11	02/04	06/01	24/02	26/08	03/02	27/01	09/09	02/09	21/04	12/09	26/12	21/10	09/12	24/03		10/03	08/08	04/11	12/08	07/04
Truro City	15/08	28/10	21/04	17/03	12/09	13/01	11/11	07/04	19/08	23/12	07/10	27/01	31/03	03/03	17/02	01/01	02/12		10/02	05/08	28/08	09/09
Wealdstone	07/04	09/09	02/12	19/08	21/04	05/08	17/02	31/03	17/03	13/01	01/01	14/08	28/08	11/11	03/03	11/09	23/12	21/10		03/02	27/01	07/10
Welling United	31/03	12/08	27/01	08/08	07/10	11/11	26/12	02/12	06/01	10/02	28/08	07/04	03/03	19/08	17/03	09/09	17/02	09/12	28/10		21/04	12/09
Weston-super-Mare	01/01	24/03	03/03	20/01	26/08	10/02	23/09	17/02	11/11	15/08	02/12	02/09	28/04	23/12	14/04	05/08	13/01	02/04	05/09	14/10		28/10
Whitehawk	04/11	06/01	26/08	18/11	10/03	24/03	05/09	08/08	26/12	24/02	21/10	02/04	09/12	14/10	12/08	02/09	23/09	20/01	28/04	14/04	03/02	

Please note that the above fixtures may be subject to change.

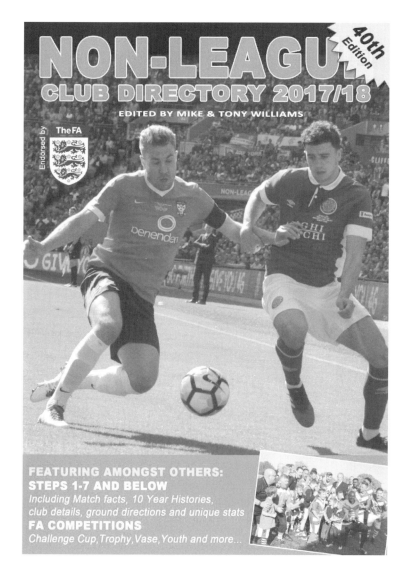

NON-LEAGUE CLUB DIRECTORY 2017/18

40th Edition

EDITED BY MIKE & TONY WILLIAMS

Endorsed by The FA

FEATURING AMONGST OTHERS:
STEPS 1-7 AND BELOW
Including Match facts, 10 Year Histories,
club details, ground directions and unique stats
FA COMPETITIONS
Challenge Cup, Trophy, Vase, Youth and more...

Now in its 40th year of publication, The Directory has developed into a comprehensive record of competitions within the non-league game and gives this level of football the publicity and prestige it deserves.

The Football Association has encouraged the development of the publication since its introduction as a small pocket book in 1978 and all their competitions such as The Cup, Trophy and Vase plus their Youth and Women's cups are featured.

Individual club pages highlight the top twelve divisions with club details, records and statistics plus senior players are featured in team photographs and within many action shots from league and cup football.

Major competitions within the nation's pyramid of domestic leagues are featured from levels 1-7 with many leagues outside of the top seven steps also featured.

Supporters' Guides and Tables books

Our Supporters' Guide series has been published since 1982 and the new 2018 editions contain the 2016/2017 Season's results and tables, Directions, Photographs, Telephone numbers, Parking information, Admission details, Disabled information and much more.

Our Football Tables books are perfect companions to the Supporters' Guides and contain historical Football League, Non-League and Scottish final tables up to the end of the 2016/2017 season.

THE SUPPORTERS' GUIDE TO PREMIER & FOOTBALL LEAGUE CLUBS 2018

This 34th edition covers all 92 Premiership and Football League clubs.   *Price £9.99*

NON-LEAGUE SUPPORTERS' GUIDE AND YEARBOOK 2018

This 26th edition covers all 68 clubs in Step 1 & Step 2 of Non-League football – the Vanarama National League, National League North and National League South.   *Price £9.99*

SCOTTISH FOOTBALL SUPPORTERS' GUIDE AND YEARBOOK 2018

The 25th edition featuring all Scottish Professional Football League, Highland League and Lowland League clubs.   *Price £9.99*

ENGLISH FOOTBALL LEAGUE & F.A. PREMIER LEAGUE TABLES 1888-2017

The 20th edition contains every Football League & F.A. Premier League final table plus play-off results and F.A. Cup and League Cup semi-final & final results.   *Price £9.99*

NON-LEAGUE FOOTBALL TABLES 1889-2017

The 15th edition contains final league tables for the National League (formerly the Football Conference) and its 3 feeder leagues, the Northern Premier League, Southern League and Isthmian League. This edition also contains tables for the Combined Counties League 1922-2017 plus, for the first time, historical notes about the National League and Northern Premier League.   *Price £9.99*

SCOTTISH FOOTBALL TABLES 1890-2017

The 6th edition contains final league tables for all Scottish Professional Football League, Scottish League, Scottish Premier League, Highland League and Lowland Football League seasons.   *Price £9.99*

These books are available UK & Surface post free from –

Soccer Books Limited (Dept. SBL)
72 St. Peter's Avenue
Cleethorpes, DN35 8HU
United Kingdom